DON'T GET A DIVORCE
MAKE MARRIAGE WORK

The
WOMAN
and the
WARRIOR

YOGA MATT

authorHOUSE®

AuthorHouse™
1663 Liberty Drive
Bloomington, IN 47403
www.authorhouse.com
Phone: 1 (800) 839-8640

Published by AuthorHouse 05/02/2018

ISBN: 978-1-5462-3452-4 (sc)
ISBN: 978-1-5462-3450-0 (hc)
ISBN: 978-1-5462-3451-7 (e)

Library of Congress Control Number: 2018903637

Print information available on the last page.

Any people depicted in stock imagery provided by Getty Images are models, and such images are being used for illustrative purposes only.
Certain stock imagery © Getty Images.

This book is printed on acid-free paper.

Dedication

*This book is dedicated to the family unit,
the foundation of our society;
to the children, our future;
to us all so that we may have
the wonderful experience that God intended.*

Table of Contents

THIS BOOK IS
DEFINITELY WRITTEN
TO PUSH
ALL YOUR BUTTONS,
AND TO MAKE
YOU THINK.

To The Reader

Each chapter that you read will be very short and contains one thought. Finishing the complete book, will help you to understand the sum of it's parts. Each piece is listed separately in the table of contents, so you can look back when you want to recall something you've read.

I hope this book will make your life easier and better.

The Woman And The Warrior

WOMAN

YOU ARE THE MAKER OF THE FAMILY.
YOU ARE THE MAKER OF THE NATION.
YOU ARE THE MAKER OF THE WORLD.
THE FUTURE OF THE WORLD IS
ENTIRELY IN YOUR HANDS.

WARRIOR

YOU ARE AGGRESSIVE BY NATURE.
YOU ARE OUT OF BALANCE FROM BIRTH.
YOU ARE WITHOUT POWER, YET EXTREMELY POWERFUL
YOU ARE THE DEFENDER OF THE FAMILY,
THE NATION, AND THE WORLD.

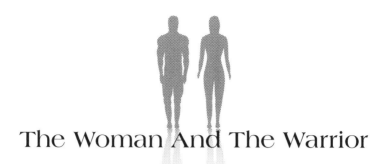

The Woman And The Warrior

For thousands of years we've followed the same course. We never questioned much about the way men and women were to function. We just said this is the way it should be, or has to be. We heard words like submit or obey, cherish and honor. We all had role models, clearly showing the way we were to act. We followed what we saw. Life seemed so much simpler then, and truthfully, a lot happier.

It's only been approximately 75 years that we've tried to change the teachings of the masters, or to rewrite the great books, without understanding what the consequences would be. All one has to do is look around to know that it has not worked.

The human being's ego is always wanting to correct or change, to control or own. The ego doesn't seem to be able to stay happy or still, so we try to take over someone else's life by physical or mental force, abusing, controlling, and by making demands of that other person. We make them feel as if they will never be happy unless they act a certain way, even though it goes against everything that they feel inside. What a way for them to live, going against their basic feelings and instincts.

The concepts of the way we were to act, the way our role models showed us, were essentially correct. We just didn't know the reasons why they did what they did. Today we're too well educated, we have too much free choice, and we're too smart to do something that we're told, unless we're given a good reason for it. If it makes sense to us, if it makes us happier, if it can put a smile on our face, then hopefully, we're smart enough to do it.

The purpose of this book, The Woman and the Warrior, is to clearly explain what our ancestors a long time ago were trying to tell us, so that a much more beautiful life can be had by all, and so that the next generation, and those to come, will benefit from the way we're living our lives in this present time.

ABRAHAM TRIED TO SAY IT. MOSES TRIED TO SAY IT. BUDDHA TRIED TO SAY IT. MOHAMMED TRIED TO SAY IT. JESUS TRIED TO SAY IT. GANDHI TRIED TO TELL US. MARTIN LUTHER KING TRIED TO TELL US. CHIEF SEATTLE TRIED TO TELL US. ST. FRANCIS OF ASSISI TRIED TO TELL US. CONFUCIUS TRIED TO TELL US. SWAMI SIVANANDA TRIED TO TELL US. MOTHER TERESA TRIED TO TELL US. IT'S IN THE BIBLE, THE COURSE OF MIRACLES, THE KORAN, THE BHAGAVADGITA, THE TEN COMMANDMENTS, AND THE LIST GOES ON AND ON. THE TEACHINGS ARE IN EVERY CULTURE OF THE WORLD. WHY AREN'T WE LISTENING?

I'm certainly not one of the above, although the great masters and teachers taught that the power to do great things is in each one of us, so I'm going to try to explain some of the teachings in my own words, the way most of us think and speak today. Because I'm just like you, maybe my words will have more meaning. I sure do hope so. I've learned a lot. I'm going to try to express what I've learned and some of the things that I feel, and some of the words I write will come straight through me from another plane. Hopefully, I can make a positive difference in your life and those around you, which will, in effect, make a difference in the future of our world.

WITH ALL THE LOVE THAT'S INSIDE OF ME,
Yoga Matt

The True Warrior

Who is this guy? Why do I call him the True Warrior? You're right ladies, he's the kind of man you fantasize about. In fiction, he might be the Lone Ranger or Superman. In history, he might have been Harry Truman or Abe Lincoln. A warrior is a good person. He's strong, not only in physical appearance, but in his actions. He stands up for what he believes is right, yet he's gentle when he needs to be. He can hug, and cry, he gets emotional, has feelings and isn't afraid to say what he thinks and feels; he's a communicator. He was brought up to be the physical strength of his family, but also is able to recognize the strength of others. He is a peaceful person, and honest, with strong moral values, but at the same time will take responsibility to protect his family no matter what. He is the man, and nobody questions that. He is a strong, centered, male figure. He's what makes the woman remain in her feminine energy, and is proud to do so.

HE LOVES HIS FAMILY AND HIS COMMITMENT IS TO MAKE SURE THAT THEY ARE HAPPY AND LOVED. When he comes home at night, it is his strength, kindness and love that makes him the true man. He is the true WARRIOR.

The True Woman

Who is this woman and why do I call her the TRUE WOMAN? It's because she's there for her family no matter what. She's a very powerful woman, make no mistake about that! As a male, I saw her many times when I was a boy. My friend's mothers were true women. My aunts were. Real women were all around me. Where is she now? She's still there, but she's the silent minority and she's becoming more the minority all the time. What a catastrophe! Thank God, as a kid, my mom was home. She was a great mom; she was a great wife. They were a team, my mom and dad. My dad never considered her a threat. She was there for all of us. She was definitely the maker of the family in all ways, and so were the other women. We had a strong nation because women used their feminine energy properly, we were much more in balance as a country. Today, our nation looks very strong on the surface; I don't know, are we strong on the inside? Only time will tell. Where are the true women that will make our world strong from their subtle energy? <u>Don't forget the future of the world is entirely in her hands.</u>

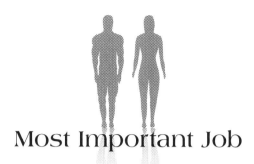

Most Important Job

What would you think the most important job in the world is? Do you think it's the person that earns money for the family? Do you think it's being president of a country? How about a priest, or a rabbi? Here's a little story that made me just want to scream out loud.

I used to attend a lot of group seminars. One day, I was sitting with a group of people on the floor, in a cross-legged position. Maybe there were two or three men out of ten people attending. The leader asked each person what their occupation was? "I'm an attorney", "I'm a doctor", "I'm a therapist", "I'm a business person", "I'm a teacher", and so on. Finally, we got to the last person. "I'm a... a... "she sort of looked down at the ground, "I'm a housewife and a mother." She was embarrassed. I almost stood up and screamed at the top of my lungs. She was ashamed of her job. I just couldn't believe it! Maybe the other people could have been embarrassed, but they sat up straight and were proud of what they said they did. This woman had the most important job of all, and the most difficult job of all. Didn't she know that? Have we lowered the position of wife and mother to that of dirt or worthless? Have we downgraded her position to that of almost nothing? Being a wife and a mother is the most important responsibility of all and that's what we're doing with it? If that's true, if that's our mentality, then we should be ashamed of ourselves and so should our whole society.

Men and women, do not buy into this garbage that being a wife and mother is not important. IT IS THE MOST IMPORTANT JOB IN THE WORLD, and it is time that we all applaud the women who have the guts to do it properly!

Thank You Mom

To all of the mothers that stayed at home to raise their kids, I say thank you from all of us. I surely know that I am a better person because you were there. Did you make mistakes? Of course you did, but on the whole, thank you. You gave us love when we came home crying. You gave us hugs when we needed them. You sometimes fought our battles when we were too small to do it for ourselves. I know that we are better people because of you.

As an adult, I know that today's society looks down on wives and mothers as doing easy, do-nothing jobs. I challenge the women to have the guts and the courage to do what you did. I challenge them to leave their high paying jobs. I challenge them to be there when their children come home from school. So many women could be at home, but they're on an ego trip for fame, and power and money. I challenge them to do the toughest, most important job of all. I challenge the men to praise the women for not shirking their responsibility, to treat them really well, to show them love and appreciation for being responsible mothers and wives. I challenge the parents in our society to spend more time with their children. I ask them to think less about their expensive cars and homes, and more about their families.

I challenge all of us to make this a better place in which to live. Hooray for the mothers of this world who are there for their children, putting their children's lives in front of their own!

My Mother's Aunt

My mother came from a family of six kids. When my mother was very young, her mother died. According to my mother, her mother's sister married her father, because it was a Jewish custom to do so. Whether true or not, it was a wonderful thing for the woman to do. She raised six children and gave them all her love. Although this was my mother's aunt, they called her mom, and all the children turned out to be nice people. The family had its problems, and in two cases really big ones, but what they also had was love, and lots of it. The family circle of energy was kept intact. While it must have been difficult, the adults seemed to do their best to put the children first. Who would do what that woman did to preserve the family, and the next generation?

SERVE, LOVE, GIVE, AND BE HAPPY

The Divine Mother

Did you ever notice how different little girls are from little boys? No, I don't just mean our physical differences, I mean the differences inside, our mind and our emotional differences. Little girls are generally much calmer, coy, sweet, and cuddly. Little boys are usually much more active, many times on a destructive level. While most girls are fascinated with dolls, stuffed animals, and playing house, most boys are usually playing with trucks, weapons of mass destruction, and toys for building.

Although these differences are fairly obvious there is one huge difference that needs special attention paid to it. The little girl is born with an invisible, feminine centering energy. It's a gift from the divine above. One name given for that wonderful, feminine, centering energy is THE DIVINE MOTHER. The Christian Religion names Mary as a symbol of that divinity within. The little girl that is born into the world, is absolutely blessed. She has something special within her for the rest of her life. Most cultures of the world knew that it was important to make sure that, at any cost, the divine feminine energy stayed within. It was known that to harm her feminine energy, to bury her divine mother, or to remove it, to take it out of the body, even in the smallest amount, was to make the girls life difficult, and to play havoc with the family, the nation, and the world as a whole. It's obvious that the little boy is born without this wonderful centering energy. Just watch the little and big boy play. Watch the young adult male and the mature male. Without something and someone to center him, the male just seems to be off balance most of the time. For the man, that something is religion, the male elders, and the woman. For the woman, that stabilizing force is the man, the women elders, and religion. Of course, most centering of all is her birthright centering energy.

So, why is our society becoming more and more chaotic? Why are people so out of sync? It's very simple if the above concept is understood. The little girl is becoming as empty as the little boy. We used to cherish the little girl for the rest of her life for her sweetness, and for her innocence. How wonderful it was to see a girl's or woman's beautiful smile, feminine look, her laughter or her tears. Today, we teach her to run like a boy, dress like a boy, play like a boy, work like a boy, act like a boy, and look like a boy. Gradually, we pull her centering energy out of her, and with that goes her smiles, her sweetness, and a reason for a real man (warrior) to want to be with her. She's now extremely competitive, dresses in masculine colors and fabrics, and works like a man. She carries a gun, divorces her husband for more independence, works in a man's world, and has sex with anyone just for the sake of fun. She doesn't know how to cook, make a home, or stay in a home. If she has children, she still wants to work, leaving the child in some kind of daycare program at a very early age. How many women would have done that just 35 years ago? With the loss of her divine mother goes her femininity. With the loss of her femininity goes her happiness, that of her husband, that of the family, the nation, and the world.

The woman's femininity today is being totally misunderstood and misdirected. It might as well be going towards some planet, in a void all the way. At any cost, it was and is important to keep the woman, from childhood on, in her femininity. Sometimes, it looked as if the woman was being suppressed. I'm not saying that raising a child is always done correctly, but the need to keep the woman in balance absolutely needed and still needs to be done. Today, we see the ramifications of a woman out of balance. Many little girls are growing up to be adults that are killing their children, deserting their husbands and children, putting their jobs ahead of their families, divorcing their husbands, and having sex with just about anyone. Some are becoming very selfish, many not willing to give of themselves, but taking only for themselves. We are teaching young girls to play sports, to swear and to destroy just like men. At the same time, more women are in jail, dying young, committing suicide, becoming alcoholics, and doing drugs, etc., etc., etc.

How Have We Gotten
Into Such A Mess?

Understand, that I am speaking out as an elder who is relying on experience, book knowledge, and intuition. I read different kinds of books, more spiritual in nature, and I sometimes seem to receive incredible channeled thoughts. I have always tried to make 2+2=4, and I've never been satisfied with anything less than the truth. I hope you find this part fascinating and I hope it shakes you up a lot!

It is only common sense that people doing equal work, whether male or female, should be paid equal wages. It is only common sense that all people should be treated with respect and love. If a woman needs to work to take care of herself and her family during difficult times, I will always understand that. That's not being selfish, that's taking responsibility. But we've gone way beyond that. We're coming now from greed, anger, ego, fear, selfishness and materialism.

Here goes! Whatever comes out ought to be inspiring to all of us. Most, if not all cultures knew that the boy, at puberty, needed to go through a male initiation. The boy needed to go through a major change, one that would teach him the responsibilities of being a man, husband, and father, so that he could take care of his family. The men were in charge of this. He needed to be strong, both physically and mentally. He had to learn how to provide for, and to protect, his family and his community.

In the early years of the child's life, it is the mother that plays the key role in bringing up that child. It's the mother's kindness, gentleness, honesty, nurturing ability, and the showing and teaching of love, that forms the child; teaching many of the wonderful values that the child will carry with him, or her, for the rest of their life. Because the mother has that centering energy inside of her, she is the one, in the early years, that usually takes that fabulous responsibility. That's why she is the maker of the family, the nation, and the world. She passes on her goodness. By the time the child is no older than seven, the child is usually completely formed on that level.

The girl should be starting to learn the responsibilities of making the home, and taking care of a family, by the mother and the other women in the community. This is done by setting a good example as well as teaching. This course never varies, and so the mother continues to teach and strengthen the young girls feminine responsibilities (energy) as she matures into womanhood.

That's not what we're doing today though. Nowadays, from an early age, we're teaching a very different story to the girl. We're giving her karate lessons. She now plays little league soccer, basketball, and baseball, and is getting interested in kickboxing and boxing. Worst of all, her coach is probably a man, teaching her the way he would teach boys. At first the girl resists, she wants to have fun and giggle and laugh and cheer, but gradually, she will conform, and little by little, a perfectly competitive male, an off balance female, is created. Her femininity is slowly being pushed aside. Her father will take her to football and baseball games, teaching her what he would normally teach his son, especially, if he doesn't have a son, or possibly if his first child is a girl. The divine mother inside is slowly being chiseled away, or smothered. As the girl gets older, we tell her to get good grades in school, so she doesn't have to rely on anyone when she becomes a woman. We tell her to do something meaningful with her life, such as becoming a lawyer, a doctor, or an engineer. We really don't want her to learn to cook in school anymore. What good will that do in a tough, competitive world. That's what she is told. Learning to cook is a waste of time. After all, money and things are what are really important; making her believe it's more important than being a wife and a mother. Take all the math and science you can. Be strong, don't get hurt when you grow up, you have to be able to take care of yourself. We push her into mixed little league athletic teams when she's younger. Why shouldn't she be able to play with boys on an equal level? We teach her how to hit hard, fight hard, play hard, teaching her to win at any cost. We gradually push her nurturing, feminine energy aside, for the so-called stronger masculine energy. We tell her, and ourselves, it's a tough world, and that she has to be able to survive.

As a woman that's just what she does, she survives. Without the divine mother inside of her, that giggle is gone; that smile disappears. She has become a man in every way, except generally her physical appearance. With her divine mother lost, or covered up, the next generation has to be even more lost than the current one. The grown woman either can't remember anymore how to teach the honesty and goodness, or selfishly just doesn't have the time anymore. She probably can't get married or stay married. What real man (warrior) would ever want to have her for his mate?

WITH HER DIVINE ENERGY LOST, THE FAMILY, THE NATION, AND THE WORLD, ARE ALSO LOST.

Religion clearly understood all of the above. Being Jewish myself, but having almost no religious education, I later in life wanted to understand some of the things that my religion taught. I have come to discover that all orthodox religions are fundamentally the most correct in all faiths but, because we've lost the purpose behind the teachings, we've pulled away, and diluted the teachings, because they seemed so ridiculous, or harsh. They all seemed to separate the women from the men in many of their spiritual services. It had to do with energy, masculine and feminine energy. If you make the man weak, depleting his masculine side, he's worthless. If you make the woman strong, by increasing her masculine energy, so is she. Don't forget, societies planned for the future, not just for today. Some planned out generations in advance for the survival of their communities.

In the Jewish Orthodox Religion, the boy and girl, sit with their mother and the other women, during religious services. The women do not sit with the men; they are separated.

When the boy reaches approximately the age of thirteen he goes through a metamorphosis of masculine energy. His voice deepens, he develops hair on his face and body, and the responsibilities, of the rest of his life, are now about to be taught and explained. It's called the right of passage, or the bar mitzvah. He now spends much more time with the men, no longer needing to be taught as much by his mother and other women. They do not clearly understand his emotional needs or feelings anymore. Even though the father should have always been there for him, the father's role increases tremendously, and so does that of the community of men. It's now time to teach the young man to understand how to use his birthright, newly discovered, strong masculine energy, not just in the sense of his appearance, but his feelings inside his heart. I will discuss more of this when I discuss the male at greater length.

Now to the young girl. She has also been raised by, and has spent more time with her mother. She is also changing around thirteen years of age. Her instincts and feelings, on an emotional feminine level, are also getting stronger. At the same time, her physical appearance is changing on that feminine level as well. Her teachers don't change. She now has to learn how to carry out the duties, of the woman, from her mother and the women of the community. If we don't teach her properly, everyone and everything suffers.

I saw an article in the newspaper a few years ago. It said that one American Indian tribe called this right of passage into womanhood, puberty rights. The man and woman go through a new growth experience; both go through a right of passage. Both, already taught mostly by the women to be good people, will now learn how to be wonderful adults, balanced with their own wonderful birthright energy.

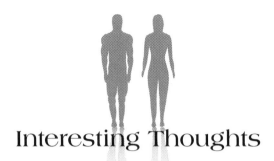

Interesting Thoughts

The following are some interesting thoughts, one liners you might say. (from the book Sthree Dharma by Swami Sivananda)

She silently rules and governs the world.
Woman is the complement to man.
She is a goddess here on earth.
Man is more rational, woman is more emotional.
Too much freedom and liberty for a woman leads to a disastrous life.
Only if she is educated, will her children be properly trained and disciplined.
The inspiring force of the woman is the home.
A woman's natural sphere of activity is the home.
Without love of God, a house is a burial ground, though it may be a palace.

Four True Stories

(turn the page and read on)

I Don't Know Who I Am
true story #1

Recently, I met a young woman. She said, "I don't even know who I am anymore, or how to act or how to think. I want to get married and have kids, but I don't even know who I am anymore. In trying to climb the ladder of what I thought I was supposed to become, I've lost myself."

Parents do not teach your daughters masculine energy, otherwise when they grow up, they may feel as if they've lost themselves. With this woman, it happened in her twenties. I find the feeling of loss of self generally happens somewhere around 35 years of age.

Woman is the energy aspect of the Lord.

Think Pink
true story #2

The year was 1991. I was certified to teach Yoga that year, at the Sivananda Yoga Retreat, in Val Moran, Canada. There I met a young woman. She was then about 27 years old. We talked a lot. She really didn't know much about how to be a woman. She had older brothers, from what I remember, her masculine energy was very strong, and she said she was always trying to keep up with her brothers when she was younger. As part of the conversation, I said that just for fun, she should wear a pink ribbon around her finger as a reminder of her femininity. We would kid about that a lot.

Sometimes, when I think about what I said to her, I think about women in general. Did they wear lace and ruffles and sashes and frilly clothing to keep themselves in their feminine energy, to feel like women? That's probably part of it. Certainly when a little baby is born, the mother can't wait to dress the baby and decorate the baby's room according to its sex.

A man has to look like a man and feel like a man, and a woman, she too, has to feel and act according to her gender. If we don't do that, we may be very unhappy when we grow up.

I Filled Your Tank
true story #3

Here's another true story to try and explain how ridiculous it can get. My friend has a date with a woman; their first date. He stops for gas, puts his credit card in the pump, and it won't accept his card. He says, "I'll be right back" to the woman and goes to the office to pay for the gas. The attendant says, "your gas is already being pumped." He gets to his car; the woman had used her credit card and was pumping the gas. She thought she was doing the right thing. He felt like a fool. He had the money, the pump wouldn't take his credit card. She needed to give him a chance to take the proper responsibility to pay for, and pump the gas. When she paid for the gas and pumped it, he certainly didn't feel like a man. I wonder if she felt like a woman?

Many men expect a woman to pay for her share of a dinner when they eat out. If he expects that on a date, he will probably expect that always. Is that the man the woman wants to be with? Women, give the man a chance to show his true colors. (A true male would prefer to pay for the meal, and in return, there isn't a man alive that wouldn't like a home cooked meal.)

Remember, the man is the natural provider/protector. If the relationship is not set up properly from the beginning, it gets harder to set it up properly later on, and will probably explode.

All Girls
true story #4

A while back, I saw a woman wearing a T-shirt that made a reference to all girls. I couldn't see the whole shirt, so I went up to the woman and asked what the T-shirt said. It was a slogan from an all girl college. She told me that her sister went to the school, and when first there, was "going to conquer the business world." You know, be a strong executive contender. After being there a while, she changed her mind. Her feminine energy got much stronger. Instead of conquering the world like a man, she wanted to conquer it with a man, and enjoy being a wife and a mother. I thought that was very interesting and it sure put a big smile on my face.

Work Day

It's called something like Parent, Daughter Work Day. It's a national day when parents that work are supposed to take their daughters with them, to show them what they do. I agree, when a child spends time with a parent that's terrific. But, there is a very strong negative side to this day. It teaches the little girl to work, generally not in a supportive role, but in the role of provider. It teaches the girl to get out of the home and into business. We teach by example. Is this the example we want to teach the future generation of women? It places masculine energy into the girl. It's what the men are supposed to do with their boys. What's good for the boy is good for the girl, right? No, not at all. The parent is now teaching and reinforcing the daughter with more masculine energy. The girl is being taught that to be approved of, respected and happy, she needs to leave the home and have a job, especially if she goes to work with her mother. She learns that she'll have to take a heavy load of academic classes in school, not to better teach her children in the early years, but to make a living. We're already convincing her that in order to be okay, she'll have to look and act like a superwoman, play and compete in men's sports, and last, but not least, to now have a career, so that she can be an independent woman and make all kinds of money. Of course, as she gets older, she will find out that all that stuff will never make her happy. Boy, are we blowing it! Eventually, the girl will discover, through her own instincts, that what she really wants is to get married, have kids, and share a wonderful life. And you know what? The men are buying into this too, thinking that this powerful woman will make their life happier also. Of course, as they both get older, they realize that this won't work, that they're both on the same side of the energy circle and that they've both been had. Not everyone, but most. To test it and to find out if you're the one that can survive going against the grain of our natural instincts, just isn't worth it. Sounds to me like it's a set up for never getting married, having an unhappy marriage, having screwed up kids, or divorce. I don't think anyone wants any of that.

THE
PROVIDER/PROTECTOR
ROLE FOR A WOMAN IS A SURVIVAL ROLE
and should only be used in time of definite need.

But

I know the male works hard to take care of his family. I know he is the provider & protector of the family, but, not to spend time with his family, not to enjoy his children, not to spend time with his wife? Not to give them special attention, not to give them lots of hugs and kisses; what's it all about? Use your head, guys. Come home and enjoy your family. Cut down on all the materialistic stuff, it's not as important as you think. (If you haven't got enough money to put a roof over their heads, or food on the table of course, that's a different story.)

LOOK BACK WITH A SMILE ON YOUR FACE, GIVE YOURSELF A PAT ON THE BACK WHEN YOU'R OLDER, AND SAY, JOB WELL DONE!

Another True Story

Special Time

I was sitting in a restaurant with my friend, when I spotted three people in a serious discussion. It was a father with his two sons. The boys were about 12 and 15 years old. I couldn't hear what the father was saying, but the boys sure were listening. I had to ask the father what they were talking about, so I did. He told me he was from South Korea, and he and the boys had a special talk for about 20 minutes every day. That day they were talking about education. "Learn all you can in school," he said, "in twenty years you'll be happy you did."

I wish more fathers and men would take that kind of special time with boys. Things would sure be a lot better if they did.

Thank You Dad

To all the men that come home to spend special time with their children, from all the children, I say thank you. It's plenty tough to be a father, but it's well worth it. When it's all said and done, it's a great ride in life to be there for your children, to watch them grow, to teach them, and to love them. Of course, men are not perfect either, but for the most part, men do love their children. Good fathers work very hard to make a living to take care of their kids, and they do their darnedest to get home for birthdays, special activities at school, and holidays, many times cutting their day short, just to be there as a sign of love, support, and smiles. Teaching kids, taking them on picnics, and vacations, that's what it's all about! Spending time with their family; being there for their kids, no matter what, that's the privilege of being a father. Talking to their daughters, being there for their daughters, hugging their daughters, always being a father to their daughters as long as forever.

Remembering to say the words <u>I love you.</u> That too is what it's all about. To their sons, still remembering to say I love you, still remembering to hug, no matter how old they get, spending time with them all the way through their lives; that's what my dad did. "Thank you Dad, you were always there for me; you spent a lot of time with me." You taught me how to work and be honest. You took me to work, and paid me, even though I knew sometimes you didn't have the money to do that. Perfect men? I don't think there are any. Great fathers? There are plenty. We just don't hear much about them because our society focuses too much on the negative. "Again, I say thank you Dad.

****To the fathers that aren't spending more time
with their kids, you're really missing out.****

IF YOU WANT A CHILD TO BE A TERRIFIC MAN OR A TERRIFIC
WOMAN, THERE MUST BE A TERRIFIC MAN AND A TERRIFIC
WOMAN TO TEACH THAT CHILD.

Follow Like Sheep

Did you ever notice how major manufacturers are designing products to win us over? Companies are designing cars, clothing, perfume, and cosmetics, with the idea of getting you to spend your money. It doesn't matter what it does to you, it matters that they have a stronger bottom line of profit. Men are wearing cologne to smell like women, dyeing their hair, and wearing colors that are feminine in nature. Macho cars and trucks are being produced in feminine colors, and styled to feel softer, trying to get more business for their company. Without us knowing it, we are going on the other side of the circle, being brainwashed by advertising. Just as women were pushed into smoking years ago by advertising, so are we being pushed in the wrong direction now. Even though we fall for the advertising, many of us know that it just doesn't feel right once we own the product. The rest follow like sheep, and society continues to go off balance. When you become aware of masculine and feminine energy, you clearly begin to know what you want, and you more or less start to think from the heart. You think more clearly on how you really want to live, and how you really want to spend your money, and you definitely become happier.

****

Right after I wrote the above piece, I was watching television. Being advertised was a type of women's clothing called power suits so a woman could compete with a man in high places. The suit looked like a man's in fabric and similar in design, but came with different length skirts, one short, one long. Makes one wonder why a woman would want a short skirt as part of a power suit. Makes one wonder why a woman would ever wear a power suit. Makes one wonder why a man would ever want to be with a woman in a power suit. (In order to be with that kind of a woman in a relationship, a man would have to become super strong to maintain his masculinity, otherwise he would probably wind up in a role reversal. A relationship like this is almost impossible to keep alive.)

Sowing The Seeds

Recently, on television, many commercials are showing women in professional roles. One possible reason is to program women to become professionals, and the other, more likely reason, may be to get women to purchase products. The brain only knows what it sees and hears. The girl, while growing up, is being taught to be a professional woman, and the boy, who is a natural provider/protector is getting mixed signals. In fact, both are getting mixed signals and both roles are being weakened. It's like people are walking in a fog not understanding what life is really all about and so we continue to make it more difficult to function as happy adults.

The strength of the nation lies in the homes of its people
Abraham Lincoln

Flour Dough

This piece comes out of the book, Sacajawea. Here the woman, Sacajawea, is speaking.

"Hee--- when I was a papoose no one thought about me walking into the river. They deliberately pushed me, and I learned to swim. We learned to take care of ourselves in those days. This boy will have soft white muscles, like flour dough. Pagh! What kind of men will women make these days? Soft like dead fish, lazy as fat cats, pale as dusty bones--that is not men, that is shadow."

As I've stated earlier, it's the women that teach the boy (and girl) the goodness, it's the men that teach him how to understand his strength, but the above says it enough; we are creating men more like flour dough. If we push the young girl into the river she will be strong, but we will be teaching her to be a survivor. Sacajawea was the only woman on the Louis and Clark Expedition.

In the same book, the male right of passage is discussed. The initiation was so severe that sometimes some indian boys did not survive. Don't forget, they were going to be the hunters and protectors of the tribe.

Mom, There's A Girl On My Team!

"My daughter goes to Harvard." "No, my son can't play football, it's too dangerous." "Isn't my son's hair gorgeous and don't you like his earring?" "My daughter just got a full scholarship in soccer." If you just stand outside the circus that we're creating, you'll probably hear conversations similar to the above. As these children become adults, this is what one might hear. "My daughter is 37 and still hasn't gotten married. She very rarely goes out with the same guy more than twice. She makes a lot of money, but she's not very happy. She'd love to get married and have a family. My son, oh, he's still living at home. I wish he'd move out, but he doesn't seem to have the desire to achieve. There seems to be something wrong with him."

Just listen and watch. This is what's going on out there in many variations of the above. We are strengthening our women with masculine energy, and we're losing our men. No man wants a woman filled with masculine energy for a wife, unless he's a weakened male. No woman wants a wimp for a mate, that's for sure. The energy circle will shatter, with sparks flying everywhere! If people get married and there is a role reversal, it will generally lead to a divorce, or a dis-ease. One or the other person will eventually get out and marry someone that will put them in their proper energy.

The latest tragedy to strengthen the women and weaken the men is mixed little league sports. When are we ever going to wake up? Men coaching girls sports is bad enough, but mixed teams? What are we doing? Why is this happening? First of all, the women's movement has gotten lost if this is one of the things they are fighting for. Secondly, divorced mothers not wanting to see their daughters suffer like they did, because of the pain of their divorce, are trying to strengthen their daughters to protect them from being hurt like they've been hurt. Would you ever put your son on a girl's team? Push the masculine energy into the girl and she will be fine - BULL! Women, would you want a man wearing pink, with a nice soft look, to protect you? Think about it. Holy Toledo! What the heck are we doing? Just look at this mess. Little boys and little girls on the same baseball team. How do you coach them? I used to coach. Coaching baseball, if done right, is not just teaching baseball, it's teaching boys to work together for the benefit of the whole. It's teaching boys to be positive, and say positive words to their team mates, and not to say nasty things to the other team. It's teaching boys to do their best, and that they can achieve what they want if they practice and don't give up. It's teaching boys to believe in themselves. It's not just teaching a sport; it's teaching sportmanship and how to be a centered adult male. It's teaching strong masculine energy, and putting it into the body and mind of the boy. Hopefully, when he grows up, he will have the confidence and strength in himself to take the male adult responsibility for his family, community, and for the next generation of kids.

Now enters a girl on the team. Teaching the boy to do his very best, to play the sport with all he has, to play honestly, but to play hard; that's good training for a boy. How can he do that if a girl is on the team? Hopefully, he will be taught to play gentler when she's receiving the force of the game. If he treats her like a boy, she will get too strong and he may never treat her with respect as a woman when she grows up. Teach him to slide in hard, and he may just do that to a woman as he gets older. He may become abusive and never give it a second thought. Come in like a wimp, and he may be too weak to protect and provide for his family. Do we want her to be filled with powerful masculine energy? Do we want him to act wimpy? The ramifications of what we are doing are mind boggling. Women are already saying, where are the true men? Men are already saying, where are the real women? Can you imagine what the next generation will be dealing with!

Do we want to override our natural, birthright, strong energy? Don't you think it's important to keep the woman in her feminine energy and the man in his masculine energy? Why are we working so hard to destroy ourselves and the next generation?

A WOMAN IS ALWAYS TESTING TO SEE IF THE MAN IS STRONG ENOUGH TO TAKE CARE OF HER ON A MASCULINE, PROVIDER/PROTECTOR LEVEL

Female Right Of Passage

Isn't she sweet? Isn't she nice? Isn't she cute? Isn't she lovely? Isn't she beautiful? Isn't she wonderful? All her life, from little girl to teenager, to woman, to senior, the female needs to hear these words. She may not admit it, and she may fight being a woman throughout her life. She may, as I said before, act like a man, but, you'd better believe inside she's a woman. She may override her emotional feelings, but if she does, inside her heart, she hurts. Her birthright is feminine energy. How dare society ever let her feel other than a woman! <u>SHE IS THE MAKER OF THE FAMILY, THE NATION, AND THE WORLD.</u> ***The destiny of the world is entirely in her hands.*** <u>How dare society ever let her feel other than a woman!</u>

I recently saw on television that tigers are on the verge of extinction. They are becoming extinct mainly because of poachers. How many tigers do you think were killed by women? In the past how many women killed, created wars, destroyed the land, etc.? But things are changing. Women today do kill, and fight in wars with rifles and bombs. Without her nurturing, nest building balance, will society survive? According to everything I've learned, feel, and believe, NO!

The girl's right of passage into womanhood takes place at about twelve years of age. A little earlier than the boys. While the young girl and boy are taught in their childhood years, goodness, kindness, love, compassion, honesty, and caring, the young woman, now at puberty continues her teachings with the women. It is extremely important to keep her in her feminine energy, her Divine Mother. That does not mean the woman is weak. It means that the young woman is feminine and is now to learn, and strengthen the responsibilities of her feminine, nurturing, and nest building centering energy. Although these abilities are instinctive, teaching and guidance by the mother, female family members, and the community of women are a necessity. She is to learn how to understand herself as a woman, how to be a good wife and mother, and how to take care of the responsibilities of the home. After all, it's the positive centering energy of the home, and the love in the home, that is of major importance to the happiness of the family. The home is the center of all activities. This is the way it's supposed to be. Making a wonderful home, and centering the family with her nurturing energy, is the most important responsibility of a woman. The home and family are slowly being destroyed. Unlike the early days, more and more activities now take place outside the home. The core place for the family gathering is disappearing.

We are stripping the woman of her importance. We are stripping the woman of her feminine energy. This is about the second generation of the woman's role in the home being less important. My father, who is now ninety five, tells me that the biggest push to the woman getting out of the home was World War II. How disgusting can you get? A war killing millions of people, and destroying lives. That war also would destroy families to come.

A major boost to increasing masculine energy in women was the cigarette commercial, YOU'VE COME A LONG WAY, BABY - a manipulation to get a woman to smoke in public, chipping away at her feminine energy, causing many women to have severe health problems or to die young. Another nail in the coffin of putting masculine energy into the woman.

Because mothers are now working, and many women are too busy with their own problems, there's just less and less time to teach the next generation of women. Schools teach very little about how to be a wife and mother, how to run a household, or about good moral values. How are the women to be taught if as girls they're out playing baseball, basketball, and soccer? All are aggressive, competitive sports, loaded with masculine energy. Many boys and girls are in aftercare school programs, or in daycare, from a very early age. Who is going to teach them to love, to be honest, to be sweet, and to be kind? The man can do some of this, and should, but by doing too much he pulls himself away from his side of the energy circle, and may eventually go into a role reversal when he picks up the pieces of the feminine side. Because the roles start to reverse, to prevent a gap in the energy circle, the marriage will start to crack, or short circuit. A breakdown in the marriage, a divorce, or disease may occur.

Fathers are very important to their daughters. They need to give them love and hugs, and time to talk, giving them a strong sense of feeling secure. If a daughter is happy with her father, it will be much easier for her to have love in her life as she gets older. She will be able to trust a man, and on top of that, she'll probably marry a man around her own age instead of a father figure. It is important that the father does not teach his daughter activities that place the masculine energy inside of her. There is a tendency to want to do this if the man does not have a son, as discussed in the chapter, Divine Mother.

Sometimes women, who are divorced, to protect their daughters, push them into the masculine energy so they don't get hurt like they did. What a mess!

Please, please, let the woman live her life in femininity.

Male Right Of Passage

I met a woman who said to me with frustration, "all men are wimps." Time has passed since that encounter. I'll have to say I was angered by what she said; yet when I thought it over, I realized there was a possibility she was right. Men certainly aren't as strong mentally as they used to be. They seem to be getting more violent and more physically abusive, all the time. That phrase, all men are wimps, really nagged at me. It disturbed me that men were getting so weak, and so abusive, at the same time. The question was, and is, why is this happening?

I know a person who is a terrific holistic healer. Years ago, he presented me with a research paper that someone had given him. As I recall it was written by two men interested in the problem of the increasingly weakened male. It was not their field of livelihood, it was their field of concern. What they found out was purely common sense, and in my opinion, as accurate as could be. The following is what I've pieced together from that research paper and my own observations.

Men have always been off balance, that I've stated, but not weak. Many, many years ago, the boy was raised in his early years by his mother and the women, but as he grew older, he spent more time with his father and the men. He would help out on the job. By helping out, he learned a trade, and was strengthened by the physical and mental toughness of the male. He worked with his father and other men on the farm, or in a store, or factory, also learning to take responsibility. He had strong male role models that set an example of how to be a husband, father and the provider for his family. When the industrial revolution happened, the man began to go to work alone. He and the other fathers left their sons with their mothers, and the women of the community, most of the day. The men were too busy making money. They came home tired, and had less and less time to spend with their boys. The boys were now 13, 14, 15, 16, 17, 18 years old, and still being raised mostly by the women. The boys were not learning to be men.

When World War II broke out most men went to war, leaving few men at home to teach the boys. As the young men were becoming weaker, the women were becoming stronger. We're probably now, in the second or third generation of a continually weakening male. Divorce is occurring because of an off balanced, weakened male. In divorce, the custody of the children usually goes to the mother. The boys don't have a chance to be a strong, centered, male figure. Many times, because of a divorce, the mother strengthens her daughter, but pampers and weakens her son. Both get clobbered as adults, not even knowing who the heck they are. With the adult community out of control, it's difficult for either child to have a chance. (The father plays a very important role in balancing out both the boy and girl in their teenage years.)

Religion, Religion, Religion

Religion is so critical to the happiness of life it's just that we didn't understand or think the teachings were important. We felt that we could do it better on our own. Well, we can't! Religion teaches a curriculum, a course to be studied constantly and repeated to make our lives better. The problem is that many teachers of religion are not doing their job. If the teachings of the past were made clear, more people might just be listening. We need to learn how to live our lives, to keep our lives in balance, and to keep our lives happy. Religion was and is the course for happiness.

The original spiritual leaders knew why. The purpose of their teachings has been lost or weakened, big time! Many spiritual leaders of today have not passed down the true purpose of those teachings, in most cases, for at least the last two generations.

All religions, in their early beginnings had a strong male right of passage. So did most, or all, of the cultures of the world. The Jewish religion has the bar mitzvah. Long ago, the American Indian had a very strong right of passage for boys as they passed from childhood into manhood. The movie, Roots, starts off with the male right of passage (initiation), and it is possible that the baptism, in Christianity, was originally the male initiation, beginning originally at puberty, and only for men.

It's a given that without a masculine strong right of passage, a strong male strengthening by the men, the community would perish. Don't forget, it was not that long ago, that the male was the hunter (provider) and the warrior (protector). If the males had given the women a male right of passage, and increased her masculine side, the balance of the community would, over time, short out and eventually disintegrate, both male and female becoming off balance. Since the woman is born with this centering goodness, she is already living religion. It is my opinion that religion was basically meant to center the male, and to keep him in balance on a daily basis. If the female was already balanced, why destroy a good thing? Also, when the male was kept in balance, the female would automatically be in balance. The energy circle was healthy and clear. The family was strong, the society was strong. For the most part, the family and the community were much happier than they are today.

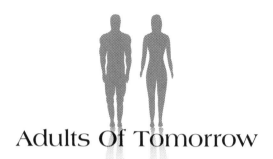

Adults Of Tomorrow

The male is the WARRIOR, the provider and protector of the family, the nation, and the world. If out of balance, he will become a destroyer, or dull, and essentially do nothing. We can see both the destroyer mentality, and the dull male, appearing more and more in our society. We have extremely aggressive males, and more homeless people than ever before. Men think big muscles, earrings, and watching sporting events on TV, just to name a few, make them men, yet inside many times, there's no substance. They are totally hollow. With few men taking time to be responsible role models, with the women's movement breaking up most male organizations, with the mother not being at home, and herself now being out of sync, we can see the huge mess that continues to develop.

For those of us lucky enough to have had a strong family energy circle, raised with good moral values, it's our responsibility to take a stand, to make a difference.

HOW ELSE ARE THE CHILDREN OF TODAY GOING TO BECOME RESPONSIBLE ADULTS OF TOMORROW WITHOUT THE ADULT'S LOVE AND PROPER GUIDANCE.

****

By the way, a country cannot have a strong society, no matter how strong its academic program is, without teaching strong moral values in school, not just at home, or in church.

It's A Matter Of Happiness

A girl and young woman needs her father. Without his love, and understanding, and talks, and time shared together she may never be able to understand and feel secure with a man. If a father is not around to show love she may search out older men to give her that completion and in many cases will marry an older man.

If there is no father hopefully there will be a man, a relative or friend of the family, that will spend time with her, so that it will be easier for her to adjust to men as she gets older.

Life Is A Circle

Life is a circle, no beginning, never ending, always changing.

Everyone travels on the circle of life, but many travel alone from the time they join the circle, until the time they leave.

Before I met you I was alone, following the rest around the circle of life.

Some traveled closely, while others were far ahead and far behind.

Some moved quickly and some moved slowly, but none traveled at my pace.

One day I saw you walk by as I was circling through life.

I noticed how similarly we moved through the circle, and I realized that we would be close for a long time.

As time went by I grew to know you, and we began sharing our thoughts and feelings.

Our stride began to synchronize, until soon we were walking side by side.

Someday, we will have a family, and our children will walk with us, until one day when they too will establish their paces, and we will be left to continue our journey together, side by side, forever.

I am giving you this ring as a symbol of the circle of life, and as my promise to <u>always</u> walk beside you.

** Written by my nephew, Kevin, and read on his
wedding day to his wife to be, Annette.**

A Relationship Contract

I NEED AN INTIMATE RELATIONSHIP AT TIMES WITH ANOTHER PERSON, IN ORDER TO BE HAPPY AND CONTENT.

I AM WHO I AM, AND WILL CHANGE WHO I AM IN THE WAY I THINK BEST. IF I CHANGE IN THE WAY YOU THINK I SHOULD CHANGE, I WILL RESENT MYSELF AND YOU.

I DO NOT WANT TO BE THE DOMINANT ONE OF OUR RELATIONSHIP, NOR DO I WANT TO DOMINATE YOU.

I DO NOT NEED YOUR CRITICISM OF ME. WHEN YOU THINK I NEED TO KNOW, TELL ME HOW YOU FEEL. LET ME DETERMINE MY RESPONSIBILITY TO YOUR FEELINGS.

I WILL TELL YOU HONESTLY WHAT I FEEL AS I COME TO KNOW MY TRUE FEELINGS.

I WILL ACTIVELY RESPOND TO WHAT I HEAR YOU TELL ME; TO HEAR YOUR FEELINGS, YOUR WANTS, AND YOUR NEEDS.

I WILL STATE MY LIMITS WHEN I CAN'T RESPOND FULLY TO YOUR EXPECTATIONS... AND TRY TO DO SO WITHOUT FEELING GUILTY.

I WILL BE AS COMPASSIONATE AS I CAN WHEN YOU ARE IN PAIN.

I WILL AVOID DOING FOR YOU WHAT YOU CAN DO FOR YOURSELF, EXCEPT WHEN IT GIVES US BOTH PLEASURE.

I WILL BE AS OPEN AS I CAN AND WILL RISK REVEALING MYSELF.

I NEED TO HOLD THAT RISKY REVELATION IN GENTLE HANDS.

I GIVE YOU THIS AS A COMMITMENT FREELY, RECEIVING YOURS.

WE HAVE A CONTRACT,

Harmony

If there is light in the soul,
there is beauty in the person.

If there is beauty in the person,
there is harmony in the house.

If there is harmony in the house,
there will be order in the nation.

If there is order in the nation,
there will be peace in the world.

Chinese Proverb

I Do, Do You?

The following are the traditional marriage vows that people have used over a long period of time. It was not easy to find the traditional vows. I phoned many places that should have known the vows. They said they could not remember them, or did not know where to look them up. Read them very carefully. They must have been worked on painstakingly by some very aware people who knew that a bringing together of two human beings was not easy, but that a separation would be even more difficult.

(VOWS FOR THE WOMAN)

DO YOU (woman) TAKE THEE (man) TO BE YOUR LAWFULLY WEDDED HUSBAND, TO HAVE AND TO HOLD FROM THIS DAY FORWARD, FOR BETTER OR FOR WORSE, IN SICKNESS AND IN HEALTH, FOR RICHER FOR POORER, TO LOVE, HONOR, AND OBEY, TILL DEATH DO YOU PART?

(woman's response)

I DO.

(VOWS FOR THE MAN)

DO YOU (man) TAKE THEE (woman) TO BE YOUR LAWFULLY WEDDED WIFE, TO HAVE AND TO HOLD FROM THIS DAY FORWARD, FOR BETTER OR FOR WORSE, IN SICKNESS AND IN HEALTH, FOR RICHER FOR POORER, TO LOVE, HONOR, AND CHERISH, TILL DEATH DO YOU PART?

(man's response)

I DO.

THE ABOVE TRADITIONAL VOWS SAY IT ALL: STAY TOGETHER. IT WON'T BE EASY, IN FACT, IT MAY BE DOWNRIGHT DIFFICULT, BUT PLEASE KEEP THE COMMITTMENT, AND WORK THE PROBLEMS THROUGH. IT'S STILL THE BEST WAY TO GO. AT ALL COSTS STAY TOGETHER, PLEASE! THESE VOWS ALSO SAY THE MARRIED COUPLE SHOULD TREAT EACH OTHER REALLY GOOD. THE MAN SHOULD CHERISH HIS WIFE ALWAYS. HE SHOULD TREAT HER LIKE A QUEEN, A GODDESS HERE ON EARTH. THE WOMAN SHOULD OBEY HER HUSBAND ALWAYS, AND TREAT HIM LIKE A KING. BOTH SHOULD LOVE AND HONOR EACH OTHER TILL DEATH DO YOU PART.

BY DOING THIS, THE MARRIAGE WILL NOT SHORT CIRCUIT AND FALL APART.

(If the man doesn't cherish her why would the woman ever obey him? These vows set up a Yin and Yang.)

One Flame

Have you ever seen the ritual in a wedding ceremony where there are three candles in a row, the outside candles already lit, the center candle to be lit by the other two candles? If you haven't seen it, you've missed something beautiful that has incredible meaning. The outside candles represent the bride and groom, the two energies of masculine and feminine that are making a committment to each other, for the rest of their lives. The middle candle is lit by both candles, creating one magnificent flame. While the two outside candles still burn, the middle candle burns even brighter, signifying two bodies, two minds, and two souls coming together to create an even greater flame, an even more incredible life experience. That's what a marriage is, two energies, masculine and feminine, coming together, to be able to reach even a further star; to be able to go beyond what they would have done alone. Don't take your marriage lightly, take it as a spiritual happening. Understand that it happened because it was supposed to......

UNTIL DEATH DO YOU PART

It Didn't Happen By Chance

Did you ever walk into a room filled with a lot of people and spend the evening talking mostly to one person? Did you ever notice that you have a lot in common with some people, and you can talk to them forever, and with other people you seem to have nothing to talk about at all? Did you ever notice that sometimes you feel like you've known a person before?

If you think that it's a fluke, that you met someone special just by chance, well maybe, and maybe not. If you marry that person, realize it's not a coincidence. There's a reason behind it, something deeper, maybe more than any one of us can comprehend. When you meet someone special, don't take it for granted. That person was meant to come into your life, two souls connecting. Today we are willing to toss a marriage, or wonderful relationship aside, thinking that it will be easy to duplicate. Well, guess again, it's not.

<u>Don't take your relationship or marriage for granted; it's special. Understand that there is a deeper meaning behind it. It did not happen by chance.</u>

Nest Builder

The woman's role of nest builder seems to be automatic. While I'm sure that there is some teaching and influence by the women, all one has to do is walk into a woman's home to see the nest builder at work. Her house is usually clean and nicely decorated, even if there is little money available. This is an instinctive role and the woman really needs to do it

Today, men can decorate because their feminine energy is stronger. They should stay out of woman's way! Don't do the decorating. It's the man's place to be the protector, checking quality, and using his strength to help out. <u>The woman needs to decorate thinking about his needs as well as her own.</u>

(When the woman has decorated her nest, she usually wants to redo it, or move and start all over again.)

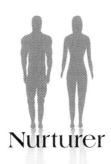

Nurturer

The woman is a nurturer. We are teaching her not to do that anymore. The end result is that we are all losing out. For the most part womens' roles, even in the work force, were supportive, or nurturing roles. Teachers, nurses, nuns and secretaries are all in that category. I agree that a woman can do anything, but at the expense of our society? Potentially without the woman in the home, the child, the man, and the family will fail. If that happens, the society will fail. That's how much power the woman has when her energy is properly directed. Her cooking, her beautiful home, her sweetness, her touches and her love give the man and the family their power.

The man should stay out of the kitchen, except in a supportive way, or when he is being the protector. He has his important role to play. He should not drain his energy, or override her energy by cooking or decorating the home.

The male needs to save his energy to be the provider, and should respect the womans' energy as it builds his strength.

Provider

To be the provider of the family is very important to the male. It is his birthright role, as well as is the protector/enfolder role. The customs of a society may be different. The male may need to be taught what those customs are. His role may need to be strengthened by the men but the man has his need to be the provider, and it is the womans need to let him do it. He needs to be the breadwinner of the family. That's why she should only act in a supportive role in helping to provide, and once he gets strong enough, she needs to relinquish the providing. If not, he will slide as his side of the circle weakens, and she may get stronger as the provider. If she gets stronger he will either have to get very strong or go into a role reversal to keep the circle from short circuiting. A role reversal generally does not work, and the relationship usually fails. It's important to keep the circle in balance with proper order.

**circle to be discussed in a later chapter.

Protector
(enfolder)

Enfolding is a notch more than protecting. It means to cover, embrace, to promote the development or growth, enclose. Man is a natural enfolder/protector of his mate and offspring. Some enfolding/protecting roles are also called male manners.

The following are just a few enfolding/protecting roles. Can you think of more?

Man is more the builder; he is interested in structural safety, strength and quality.

A man, on reflex, will jump in front of his mate and family to protect them.

He will open the door.

He will lead through a crowd so as to protect his mate.

He will wrap his arms around her, her head coming to his chest, and console her.

He will walk with her in a dark or desolate area.

He will allow her to take the seat if there is only one seat.

He will drive the car when together.

He will be the security and strength of the family on a physical level.

When standing together, if holding each other, he will normally put his arm around her shoulder, hers around his waist, so that he can enfold her, pulling her into his chest.

He will lead in dancing.

He will lead in time of danger.

He will walk on the curb side of the street, or sit on the aisle seat, the end seat.

He will try to keep her dry in the rain, at the expense of himself.

These are just some of the enfolding/protecting roles that we no longer teach. Without these being used, neither person feels important. Without giving and receiving these, plus others, both the man and the woman will eventually starve to death.

The enfolding/protecting roles help to keep the woman on her side of the energy circle, and the man on his side. They are not foolish, they are important. I know that a woman knows how to use a screwdriver. This is a small protector role. Let him do the job, because as a man he needs to.

A Few Thoughts

Not only is the woman the nest builder and nurturer, she is also the social organizer. This may even be part of the nurturer role. The woman is usually the one that initiates most of the social activities that the couple or family will do, including eventually, who many of their friends will be. Of course, everything needs to be discussed by both, but the woman generally organizes the activities, not the man. (In the early days of dating, it's the male that plans the activities. As the relationship becomes more secure, he will ask the woman what she wants to do to make her happy assuming the protector role.) When the male's energy is devoted to provider and protector, the woman usually becomes the social organizer. It's just an automatic shift.

While we're on the subject, without the woman's nest building energy, men would just have a place in which to live, instead of a wonderful home. Men are not the nest builders! If a man is a terrific homemaker and decorator of their home, the energy circle starts to be thrown in role reversal. Since it is out of balance, a possible divorce can occur.

<u>Man is not a social animal in the same sense that a woman is, and cannot be expected to be so.</u>

A Gift Story

Sometimes someone says or does something that sort of comes out of nowhere. You can't take it for granted, for it was meant to be. The following piece fits so much what I am trying to say in this book. This story is called ON COURAGE, but to me it is so much more. Here's exactly how it is written.

"So you think I'm courageous?" she asked.
"Yes I do."
"Perhaps I am. But that's because I've had some inspiring teachers.
I'll tell you about one of them. Many years ago, when I worked as a volunteer at Stanford Hospital, I got to know a little girl named Liza who was suffering from a rare and serious disease. Her only chance of recovery appeared to be a blood transfusion from her five-year-old brother, who had miraculously survived the same disease and had developed the antibodies needed to combat the illness. The doctor explained the situation to her little brother, and asked the boy if he would be willing to give his blood to his sister. I saw him hesitate for only a moment before taking a deep breath and saying, "Yes, I'll do it if it will save Liza." As the transfusion progressed, he lay in a bed next to his sister and smiled, as we all did, seeing the color returning to her cheeks. Then his face grew pale and his smile faded. He looked up at the doctor and asked with a trembling voice, "Will I start to die right away?"

Being young, the boy had misunderstood the doctor; he thought he was going to have to give her all his blood."

****

*At a very early age not only was this boy the brother, he was also the protector. That's how it's supposed to be. A man should be willing to give up his life to save a woman. It's called chivalry. All men have it, it's instinctive. It's what the young man did in the movie Titanic, to save the woman's life at the end of the movie. Women love that part because they know it feels right to them. It's in the heart of the boy, but we're not bringing it out anymore. A man should take the bullet to protect his wife, his family, his community, his country. We need to teach that again. A man should give his seat to a woman, open the door for her. He needs to be the protector, the defender, if our society is to be in sync again.

The above story came out of the book, Chicken Soup for the Soul. It certainly was a gift to me and my book.

WOW

<u>THE WOMAN IS THE BALANCE TO MAN; THE MAN IS THE BALANCE TO WOMAN.</u> A JOINING OF TWO PEOPLE IN MARRIAGE, ENERGIES BEING OPPOSITE, WITH NO GAPS, IS A COMPLETED ENERGY CIRCUIT, LOOKING SOMETHING LIKE A CIRCLE

****

If the woman stays on her side of the energy circle, and the man stays on his side of the circle, life is easy to understand, and wonderful. (Only in a short term need, or an emergency situation should we leave our side of the energy circle. If we don't get back on our side of the circle within a reasonable amount of time, a short circuit can start to take place. Many problems may start to develop including illness and/or divorce.)

The Energy Circle

Like auras, sexual energy, radio waves, cellular phone waves, and gases in the air, the energy circle does exist. It's not visible unless understood, but one can feel it. You can feel that it's not working and you can feel it when it's working well. Let me try to identify the circle, so you can also see it.

I am me and I have an energy about me. My strong side is masculine energy. I love who I am as a male; I feel the energy. I've had it my whole life. Sometimes, I've tried to override, or suppress it, to make other people happy, but I've never been happy that way and have always returned to my strong side. I've learned over the years how important it is to me, and to those around me, and I am determined not to let anyone try to steal it away from me again. It's my birthright gift. I'm talking about my wonderful, masculine birthright half, of the energy circle.

I try to keep women on their side of the circle. It seems to make them happier. Since the circle is in constant motion, it's important to notice when things have moved, to see and feel the circle, and make sure that balance is restored as quickly as possible.

Man's birthright gift as a male is being the provider and protector (enfolder). These roles only kick in when the balance of the other side of the circle is there, otherwise man is mostly in a survival mode. (Men do very poorly as either a nurturer or a nest builder, although they may go into their feminine side and try.) Woman's birthright gift is being the nurturer and the nest builder. Anything other than that will put her in a survival mode as well. If needed, she can do the job of provider and protector, although it will be a survival role.

When we are without a mate, we are very much in a survival mode. When we meet someone, it's important to relinquish our survival roles, as now we will be in balance naturally. Sometimes because of materialism, or ego, we just can't seem to let go of the other side of the circle. A power struggle and unhappiness will usually occur.

So what does the energy circle look like?
On the next two pages you will see examples
A, B, C, D, & E.

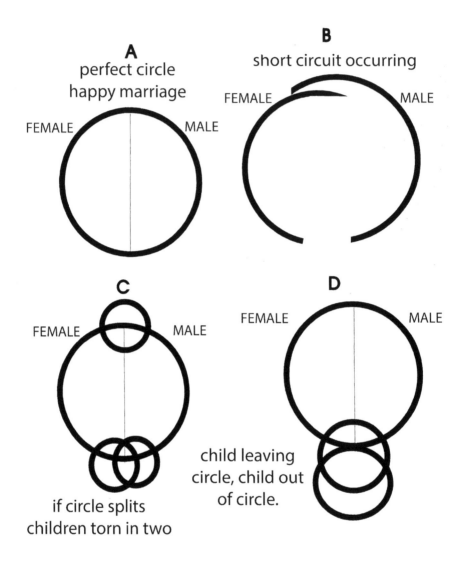

A
perfect circle
happy marriage

FEMALE   MALE

B
short circuit occurring

FEMALE   MALE

C
FEMALE   MALE

if circle splits
children torn in two

D
FEMALE   MALE

child leaving
circle, child out
of circle.

Diagram A
(turn page)

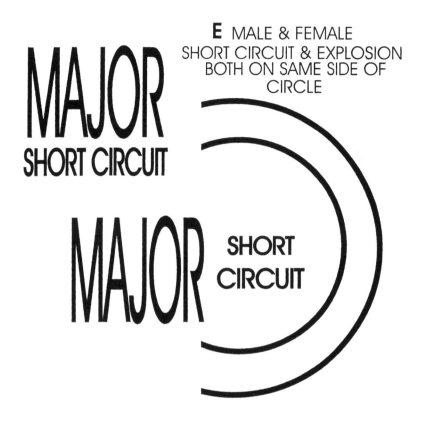

MAJOR
SHORT CIRCUIT

MAJOR SHORT CIRCUIT

E MALE & FEMALE
SHORT CIRCUIT & EXPLOSION
BOTH ON SAME SIDE OF
CIRCLE

NO ENERGY CIRCLE EXISTS
BOTH ARE ASSUMING THE SAME ROLE

Diagram B
(Turn page Circle explanation)

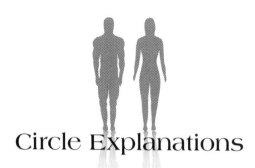

Circle Explanations

<u>A</u> is a perfect circle, the two halves meeting perfectly. If the halves are in perfect balance, then the relationship works easily. (Don't be concerned about a perfect circle, that's the ideal but not alway possible. Just create as perfect a circle as you can, and try to keep the masculine and feminine as balanced as possible.)

<u>B</u> is an out of balance circle. You can see one role taking over the other and a gap, or short circuit occurring. To stop the short circuit, the person will have to go back to their original side (role), or the side being encroached upon will have to come over to the other side to fill the gap. Keep slipping over for a long period of time, and someone will eventually blow, as a role reversal continues to happen.

<u>C</u> is a circle with a young child. Notice that the child is on both sides of the circle. If a divorce occurs the child is torn in two.

<u>D</u> is a circle of children that are leaving the nest and are going out on their own. They will soon form their own energy circle with a mate, but their circle will still touch the original. No one will ever fully leave the energy circle until a death occurs.

<u>E</u> shows a major crack in the circle. A powerful short circuit will occur, and as a result, the circle is exploding, and both people are torn apart; when this happens a divorce, disease, even death can occur. This major explosion can be prevented, if one understands and sees the breaking down of the circle, before the break gets too large, or lasts too long.

**A major short circuit can be prevented by
understanding and staying within our roles**

A HAPPY
RELATIONSHIP & MARRIAGE

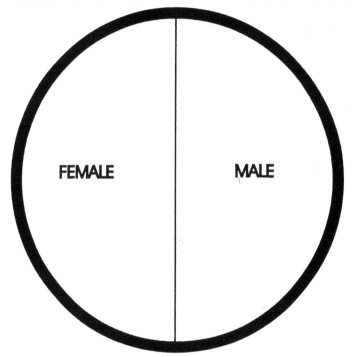

**REMEMBER TO LOVE & RESPECT EACH OTHER
FOR OUR BIRTHRIGHT ROLES!**

Diagram C

True Love

True love comes from the heart. The mind tries to reason and control it, it cannot. The heart controls all the true emotion, the mind does not. The heart is impregnable. The mind fights with all its power to change that; unhappiness occurs, sleepless nights, stress and pain. When a child is born, it is loved from the first second of life. Through pain and sorrow, all kinds of hurt, the love will not leave. The heart always accepts and bounces back no matter how hard the mind fights to gain control. Love comforts at night, it makes a wonderful day, life has meaning. The idiosyncrasies and differences are accepted, the hurts in life are corrected, the pain diminishes or disappears; the communication has to happen. The mind tries to forget; it cannot, the heart has all the strength. My mind fights you, my heart cries out for you. My heart accepts all that you are and loves every inch of you. Thank God my mind cannot win. Thank God my heart is so strong that I must write my feelings to you. My heart loves you, that means every cell in my body does too. Thank God, I have a heart.

I love you,

I didn't know what I know today. We never got married. The circle was always going out of balance. We finally wound up in a role reversal, the relationship exploded and ended.

A Balance Of Power

Man to woman, woman to man, is a perfect balance. If we work together well, we are in perfect harmony, and life is really terrific; the woman coming from the nurturing/nest building energy, and the man coming from the provider/protector energy side. As long as we stay in those birthright roles, there is no power struggle. If God is brought into our lives, and we live according to teachings like the Ten Commandments, the whole family will have a pretty darn good life. Of course, society is pulling us every which way, trying to force us out of our roles, to abuse the truths, and to damage the energy circle, so that we can have prestige and things, whether they make us happy or not. Don't get caught up on an ego trip. The happiest way is the most basic way. The more we connect with the truth, be it nature, diet, relationships, the fundamentals of religion, the happier we will be.

<u>Don't forget the woman, in her balanced, quiet, subtle energy, is extremely powerful. The man, in his balanced, noticeably strong, centered energy, is also extremely powerful. Both are needed to work together to create a strong, powerful, wonderful reaction. Opposites do attract. When they come together and work in harmony, incredible things will happen.</u>

WOMEN, UNDERSTAND THAT YOU ARE EXTREMELY POWERFUL ONLY IN YOUR SUBTLE, FEMININE ENERGY.

<u>Some one I know called this a division of labor. How about a labor of love?</u>

Opposites

Everything has an opposite. How many can you think of? Let's just have a little fun and list a few:

BLACK/WHITE
NIGHT/DAY
SUNRISE/SUNSET
UP/DOWN
TOP/BOTTOM
NEAR/FAR
YIN/YANG
MAN/WOMAN
BOY/GIRL
YES/NO
FRONT/BACK
LEFT/RIGHT
AM/PM
CREATIVE/ACADEMIC
POSITIVE/NEGATIVE
STRONG/WEAK
EMOTIONAL/RATIONAL

The list could go on and on. The above are just a few opposites off the top of my head.

****

70

A good relationship needs it's opposite energy to work. The more perfect the opposite energy, the stronger the relationship will be. For instance, I am a strong male figure, but not super strong. My masculine side needs a strong feminine energy, but not super strong, to balance me out. If I have someone who can keep me in balance I will be happy, and climb the highest mountain, so to speak. My masculine energy will balance her feminine energy out. She also will be happy, climb the highest mountain, so to speak.

The energy circle will not stay in balance without the two opposite sides, masculine and feminine both doing their very, very best to keep the circle in balance. **If someone goes off their side of the circle, someone will have to go off the other side to plug or fill the void.** It's important to understand the concept, so that the relationship hums along. **The circle has a strong and weak side, but in the weakness is the strength, and in the strength is the weakness.** Again, understanding this, will help to keep the circle balanced. Half a circle standing alone creates a major difficulty.

****

LOVE BEAUTIFIES THE GIVER AND ELEVATES THE RECEIVER
Swami Sivananda

**TO GET THE FULL VALUE OF JOY
YOU MUST HAVE SOMEONE
TO DIVIDE IT WITH.**

Mark Twain

Love Is All There Is

There is no true opposite of LOVE, since Love Is All There Is. What we think as the opposite, the word hate, is really IMAGINARY FEAR. So then, one might say the opposite of love is

fear.

Hats

To have the right to vote, to get credit in her own name, to buy a house; I remember those were important issues for women to fight for. Equal rights under the law! Our constitution provides for those rights and they should have always been had. We're not fighting for those anymore, we're fighting for the way men and women exist. We're undermining the family and the laws of nature in every way possible, without understanding why. We're just doing it. It's absolutely getting totally out of control, and the end result is that children, like I may have said before, are becoming nuts from our childish antics. The adults are acting like spoiled brats. It's what you have, I want, even if I'm not happy with it when I get it, just to prove a point. The kids are showing us we're losing it!

Women that are trying to be mothers and wives, and have a job on top of that, have a tough deal. They have to be in the masculine energy while at work, and then come home and take on the feminine energy and be the mother and wife again. Those of you who are doing that, know exactly what I'm talking about. It's like doing a hat trick. Wearing one hat during the day and one at night. It's almost impossible, and everyone is suffering because of it. If you don't have to work, don't. Buy less stuff. Your family wants love, anyhow, not stuff. Believe me women, when you look back on your life, you'll be happy you made the choice that your main job was your family.

<u>If the men don't come home, and spend more time with their children and their wives, then when they look back, they'll know they've lost out too.</u>

WOMEN, BE WOMEN AGAIN;
MEN, LEARN HOW TO BE MEN AGAIN.

I Am An Attorney

I was having a conversation one day with a friend. We were talking about women. He was speaking of a woman he used to date. What he said will stick in my mind, probably forever. He said, "I am an attorney. Why would I ever want to marry an attorney?" What he said was very profound. He wanted the opposite side of the circle of energy. He wanted a balance to his masculine energy. He eventually did get married, to a nice, kind, sweet, soft, feminine woman. She was a mate, not a business partner. He completed his energy circle, and so did she.

Two Can Play The Game

If one person understands the circle of energy keeping it in balance can work, but it's much harder to do. If both husband and wife understand the circle, then that's absolutely wonderful.

To point the finger at the other person, and not to be willing to look at ourselves, doesn't make sense. If we are both willing to work on the issues, keep the commitment to the relationship, understand that the relationship is teaching us all the time how to become better people, and that both people came together to be teachers to the other, then the relationship will last. The circle will become very healthy, and life will become very beautiful to whomever comes in contact with you and your circle.

Don't allow yourselves to buy into the game of divorce; it's become a disease, where there are few winners.

<u>If one speaks, speak with positive thoughts. To knock the other person down has no value except to destroy.</u>

Setting The Tone

The male keeps the energy circle in balance. It is he, who, with his strong masculine energy, sets the proper order of the energy circle. Don't forget, the woman is the power, but she does not set the order. That's why some societies are in trouble nowadays. With the male being weak, and out of balance, we are all out of sync. It is so important to know our roles. The woman will always be balanced as long as the man's leadership is strong, with a true centered masculine energy.

There are many places I could have put this chapter, and I know I'm repeating myself, but this is so important. If the male was in balance on a mental, physical, and spiritual level, coming from strength, not weakness, there would have been absolutely no reason for the women's feminist movement to have been created. On top of that, if started, it would have been stopped, immediately by men. Men have been so out of balance for so long, because of poor male leadership, that the woman was able to overcome the male's weakened position and start eroding the male's strong side of the circle. With the woman in the strong role, you can absolutely see society breaking down; everything is getting out of kilter.

Women, please stop trying to infiltrate the men's organizations. These organizations were and are meant to strengthen and balance the male. It may be legal to break up these organizations, but it's becoming a national disaster. Men, we have to start teaching the boys, again, to be strong centered males. If not, life will continue to get more difficult for all of us. The Million Man March was clearly a beginning of this movement. Men gathered peacefully; fathers gathered with their sons. The Peace Keepers are another good beginning. Men need to continue to have men's gatherings, combining all men's efforts, not separating them. Both efforts did not include the total population of men.

The women also need their organizations. I hope the men are not trying to break them up. If the men do get stronger, they will, as a backlash, start to infiltrate the feminine organizations, because, according to law, they also discriminate. The women need to teach the women to be women again. Men certainly don't need to break up the women's organizations, if that's what they are doing.

The Power Of A Woman

In her so called weak, submissive, supportive feminine energy, is her strength, and her power. Remember, she is the maker of the family, the nation, and the maker of the world. The destiny of the world is entirely in her hands. Her fabulous power is a very subtle energy. It's just not obvious, and was never meant to be. Today, this wonderful, life giving powerful energy is being very much misdirected, and in many cases destroyed.

Without the woman at his side, the man is off balance. He is very much weakened. His purpose in life disappears. The woman is the battery in the flashlight. When the battery is not in the flashlight, or the battery is weak, the light of the flashlight either won't turn on, or it gets extremely dim. It is her power, directed properly, that gives the man his true purpose. It is her energy that causes the man to stay in balance. The man may take the bows for what he has accomplished, but it is her tremendous nurturing, nest building energy that causes him to succeed.

When the woman's energy is not focused properly, the man is not balanced, over time he generally makes all kinds of irrational decisions. With his balance gone: with the woman's energy being either completely, or mostly misdirected, the man begins to lose it. His ability to provide for the family may slow down or completely stop. He may become an alcoholic, a drug addict, or abusive. Without the balance he will probably gather again with other men, possibly run in a gang of some kind, and in a very few instances even create a war. When his balancing energy is gone, when his purpose in life is gone, or weakened, by not having the provider, protector responsibilities, in many cases, he falls apart.

Without the woman there is no home, and little to no family life. There is very little social life and tremendous loneliness for the male. Without the woman's strength of her nurturing, nest building energy, the male may actually start to wander, and becomes a drifter.

If the child grows up without the mother's teachings, and her showing by example her goodness and kindness, the child's going to have a much more difficult time as he or she gets older. Without the divine centering goodness of the mother, and the women of the community, in the early years, the child will probably grow up misguided, which will eventually lead to a local, national, and world problem.

THE WOMAN TRULY CAN MAKE OR BREAK THE WORLD.

So how does the woman deal with all of this? She's being taught to achieve at all costs. Yet, all she ever really wants to be is a woman. Does she really want to be pushed into that masculine energy? If she does, who will she marry, and believe me, she wants to get married. Hopefully she will marry someone that will put her back into her feminine energy. That means that if she is so high up the ladder in power and position, she will have to marry someone in a stronger position than herself, generally with a much bigger ego. That kind of strong figure is very difficult to find and live with. She certainly has a much tougher time being happy. He will certainly have to work a lot harder to keep the energy circle balanced. There will probably be an invisible, or visible, constant, power struggle. Someone will eventually give out.

Women have always excelled to great heights, but mostly in supportive roles, if married, and certainly, in more nurturing roles. It isn't that women can't be anything that they want to be, but to have a society that's on a strong foundation, it's much more important for her to come from her feminine side. People of the past generations understood that they had to take responsibility in their lifetime, so that the next generation would be brought up with proper values. Society and religion taught this and traditions were passed on. In other words, the past generations were a lot less selfish, and much more connected.

Power

I keep hearing inside my head, explain this power thing further, because it's so important to understand. First, understand, there is no weak power. Both masculine and feminine energies, (or powers), are strong as long as used properly. We are all so worried about who will get the glory or accolades, that we don't allow ourselves to come from our true birthright gift.

The masculine energy is much more physical. All one has to do is watch a little boy, he just seems to want to bang and hit and shove just about everything in sight. Boys always seem to be checking out their strength and checking out their bulging muscles. As I've said in this book in other chapters, girls have a much more subtle energy. They generally play more quietly. All one has to do is watch to see the difference. Many girls do go through that tomboy stage early on, and seem to want to play with the boys, but my recollection is that it goes away fairly quickly.

A man's skin is rough and appears harder; a woman's skin is smooth and softer. There are two opposites right there. That's the circle right there, the strong and the weak side. Now don't roll your eyes and tell me I'm nuts. If you stop and think, you know it's true. We definitely are being misled from all directions, and ruining our lives by thinking we can do it differently. Most of us are created a certain way, which is a blessing, and yet, we are all working so hard to destroy our true nature by overriding our birthright heritage.

The physical power of a man is not any stronger than the subtle power of a woman, it just appears that way. Women that are really connected to their feminine energy know how powerful they are. They're confident, content and happy with who they are, and wouldn't have it any other way. Many of the women who have gone more into the masculine side, wish they could go back to their feminine side. So many women are leaving their husbands, thinking that their life will be better, only to find out that they've been hoodwinked.

The man is the provider/protector of the family, he should drive the car when together, he should wear strong colors, and he shouldn't live in the kitchen. He should be in the garage cleaning it out, he should be changing the tire, he should be carrying the money in his pocket, and paying the check in the restaurant, he should be making the living to take care of his family. The woman will love and respect him more if he does this. Does a woman really want to be married to a wimp? The man should come home and love and appreciate the woman more than anything for her subtle, powerful, feminine energy. That's the mistake we all make. Folks, love each other physically with hugs and kisses, and verbally and mentally with kind positive words and thoughts for staying on your birthright side of the circle, so that your life works in harmony. I know the energy circle is always moving, but stay on your side as much as you can. Don't fall into the trap that we're being manipulated into and screw up your life. I hope I've cleared up any of your thoughts on this topic. If not, I've sure tried.

Where there is love, there is peace and harmony.

Swami Sivananda

Stuff

The biggest reason that we may be screwing up our lives is that we want "stuff". Things, ya know? Bigger homes, more expensive cars, expensive clothes. As you get older, you know you've been had. "Stuff" will never make you happy. Just ask the person that got "stuff" in place of love. If you get the "stuff", fine, as long as it's not important to you and as long as the love comes first. If you're not there for your family and for one another, then what's the point of having the stuff? This reminds me of someone I met who had a huge home with an elevator in it. She was divorced and unhappy. Or the man who had a huge home with a tennis court. He sat down right in the middle of the court and cried; he didn't even play tennis. I have heard these kinds of stories so, so many times.

The Woman Is Not A Warrior

A girl, (or boy), goes to the movies or watches TV and what the senses pick up, in many cases, is how they will function in their lives. <u>What goes into the mind over and over again, will eventually be recreated by the mind, and carried out into reality.</u> That's a given, and has been known for thousands of years. So, knowing that, let's make the woman an Amazon, and the man wimpy and weak. Let's make her the destroyer, mean, nasty, Goliath in strength. Let's show her using guns, and doing all kinds of physical fighting. In fact, let's show her being able to fight three, no, four men at one time. Let's make her the most physically strong woman that has ever lived.

Do I really need to write any further? Today, many women actually believe that they can outpower men, on a physical level. This is what we're teaching, and this is what we are believing, but in real life, it's just not true. It just doesn't work that way.

Two warriors coming from the same side of the energy circle, oops, excuse me, there is no circle. There's only half a circle with a big, wide open gap. No circle, no relationship, unless someone is willing to pick up the missing half. If the man goes to the feminine side - no good. If the woman stays where she is, and the male gets stronger, he will have to be beyond strength - again, no good.

The woman is not the physical warrior, so why is it that we are trying so hard to convince her that she should be that way? Two warriors and nobody's at home. Two warriors usually create a divorce, or a very difficult relationship.

Submit

How can such a little word create such a big noise? It is absolutely mind boggling how we get so caught up on words. For instance, nowadays we make a big thing out of the word girl. Years ago, if a woman was called a girl, or if a woman was going out with the girls, it basically meant that no matter how old the women were, they were still young at heart, or still looked their youth. To be called a woman sort of meant a sign of getting old. That's the way I remember it as a boy. My mother always went out with the girls; she always talked about the girls, even at age ninety. To her it wasn't an insult, it was wonderful, and it was fun. Today, if a person uses the word girl in place of woman, it's almost considered disgraceful.

Maybe the same thing holds true for the word submit. It's an old word. It's been around for a long time. It's in the Bible. Is it possible that the meaning is now quite different? In today's dictionary, the definition is to yield, or surrender oneself to another. It comes from the Latin language meaning to place under. The word submissive means to become docile; a meekness. Sounds pretty bad, but maybe not.

The word is very strong, but may have been needed to explain the balance and power of the energy circle. The word may have been trying to establish an order in the way a man and a woman, husband and wife, could function at their best, preventing a short circuit from occurring. (An opposite word to submit really doesn't seem to exist that makes any sense at all. One person I know says the woman is to submit to man, and man is to submit to God. At least that makes sense.)

If the woman is to put and keep herself on the opposite side of the energy circle, then the opposite word for submit might be cherish, respect, and or love, otherwise, why would she ever submit? Why would she ever put herself in the so called "weak" position, allowing the male to be in the so called "strong" position, and be abused? She is putting the energy circle in balance by taking her birthright feminine role. If she is to be soft and full of sweetness, then he'd better be fully willing, from his heart, to completely cherish, respect, and love her. If he wants to be treated like a king, then he had better, absolutely, treat her like a queen.

THE WOMAN, BY SUBMITTING, KEEPS THE ENERGY CIRCLE IN BALANCE SO THAT THE RELATIONSHIP WORKS. <u>THEREFORE, TO SUBMIT AND TAKE THE OPPOSITE SIDE OF THE CIRCLE IS NOT A SIGN OF WEAKNESS, BUT A SIGN OF TREMENDOUS STRENGTH.</u>

***Read the chapter, Power Of A Woman.

Supportive

Maybe the word wasn't submit after all, maybe the word was supportive. It seems to me, when I was beginning my search for the truth, I read an English language version of the Old Testament. In fact, I know I read these words, "The woman is to play a supportive role to the man." When I first read those words, I was in shock, just like so many other things I've read or heard that have shocked me, until I was able to figure them out. If the idea of the energy circle is true, if the woman goes to the strong side of the circle, not being supportive, but being the main figure; if she plays the strong side, and the male plays the strong side, a total collapse of the energy circle will be created. If the male goes to the weak side, to keep the circle complete, both the woman and the man eventually will be unhappy, as a role reversal will eventually take place. In either case, a short circuit will occur, and a breakdown of the marriage, or relationship, will probably follow.

When two people support each other, one from the masculine and one from the feminine side, using their own birthright energies, the circle is extremely strong. The energy is so powerful that the relationship will soar to tremendous heights in all aspects of life.

By the way, the woman is <u>always</u> testing the male to make sure he is strong enough to take care of her on a provider, protector level.

<u>*MARRIAGE IS NOT A PLACE TO STAND UP FOR YOUR RIGHTS. MARRIAGE IS A DECISION TO SERVE THE OTHER.*</u>

*** Read the chapter, THE POWER OF A WOMAN.

Woman is the helpmate of man
behind every great man is a woman

I Am The Man

I suppose women think it's easy for the man to be the man. Well it's not, but it's easier for us than it is for the woman. We have the need to take care of a family, but you know we love doing it as long as the woman is supportive with her feminine energy. We need our back rubbed, some good lovin', a home cooked meal, and not much more, not everyday, but sometimes. For that, we'll do just about anything she wants. We don't want a power struggle, we want a balance.

If we are a good guy we don't hang around with our buddies most of the time. We can be somewhat boring, but we sure do love our families. We're actually easygoing as long as the feminine energy balances us out, and as long as nice things are said between both of us. (Why would anyone say nasty words anyhow?)

Sometimes we need to be with the guys, just for a break, but, if we get that love at home, we really don't need it anywhere else. That brings me to another point. As men, sometimes we need to be just with the guys to strengthen our masculine energy. The problem is that some women just don't want us to. Years ago, that would never have been tolerated because the male was too strong. It seems to me, women need their women's leagues, women's groups, and women's clubs, but many women sure don't want us to have our men's groups. I'm talking about groups such as little league sports, men's colleges and schools, male clubs, the military and even where we work. How are men ever going to maintain, or teach the masculine responsibilities if there is no sanctuary for them to do it in.

The woman has such powerful feminine energy. One woman in a room full of men will change the focus of the masculine energy almost immediately. If a woman has a son, she will hopefully want the men's organizations, especially if he has no father. Where else is he going to learn to be a man, but from men. Many of the women I know say, where are the men?

We're not even allowed to make men anymore. That's, again, why the men are weak, soft, wimpy and feminine. And, of course, look at the women. A lot of them are strong, and abusive, and in many cases unhappy, lonely and miserable. What a mess!

Men generally do not gather unless the gathering is organized - gangs, wars, spiritual services, sporting events, card games, are some examples. Otherwise we are loners. Just look at the men in restaurants. We sit alone, one after the other. It's only the young man that still spends time with his friends on a daily basis. As we get older, that type of gathering stops. To get one guy to go out for dinner is almost a miracle unless it's a business meeting. To get more than one guy to go out socially is almost impossible. Not so for the women.

The men need their men's organizations. Without them, we will lose our men and see more crime and more feminine energy coming from men. SINCE THE MEN SET THE ORDER OF THE WAY THINGS WORK, DESTROY THE MEN AND EVENTUALLY THE WOMEN ARE DESTROYED AS WELL.

But

I know the male works hard to take care of his family. I know he is the provider & protector of the family, but, not to spend time with his family, not to enjoy his children, not to spend time with his wife? Not to give them special attention, not to give them lots of hugs and kisses; what's it all about? Use your head, guys. Come home and enjoy your family. Cut down on all the materialistic stuff, it's not as important as you think. (If you haven't got enough money to put a roof over their heads, or food on the table, of course, that's a different story.)

LOOK BACK WITH A SMILE ON YOUR FACE, GIVE YOURSELF A PAT ON THE BACK WHEN YOU'R OLDER, AND SAY, JOB WELL DONE!

(purposely repeated)

"If you give a 7-year old the choice of tossing a ball with Dad or playing a computer game, it's the rare 7-year old who doesn't choose tossing the ball."

Dr. Gwen Wum
From the Miami Herald, Living and Learning section, Nov. 26, 1999
Article by Donna Gehrke White

It's the simple things in life that make us happy, like spending time with Dad, and playing outdoors. Remember, "stuff" will never make a person happy. It's the <u>love</u> that counts.

The Way Of Love

If I speak with human eloquence and angelic ecstasy but don't love, I'm nothing but the creaking of a rusty gate.

If I speak God's Word with power, revealing all his mysteries and making everything plain as day, and if I have faith that says to a mountain, "Jump" and it jumps, but I don't love, I'm nothing.

If I give everything I own to the poor and even go to the stake to be burned as a martyr, but I don't love, I've gotten nowhere. So no matter what I say, what I believe, and what I do, I'm bankrupt without love.
    Love never gives up.
    Love cares more for others than for self.
    Love doesn't want what it doesn't have.

Love doesn't strut, doesn't have a swelled head, doesn't force itself on others, isn't always "me first," doesn't fly off the handle, doesn't keep score of the sins of others, doesn't revel when others grovel, takes pleasure in the flowering of truth, puts up with anything, trusts God always, always looks for the best, never looks back, but keeps going to the end.

LOVE NEVER DIES
Trust steadily in God, Hope unswervingly, Love extravagantly

from the book, THE MESSAGE
by Eugene H. Peterson
(the New Testament, Psalms and Proverbs in Contemporary Language,
I Corinthians 13)

IF YOU ARE MARRIED,
STAY MARRIED.
THIS IS THE MASTER'S
COMMAND, NOT MINE.

Women Should Never
Work For Money

If the above title didn't push all of your buttons, I don't know what will. The first time I saw those words written down I thought the author was nuts. Another thought is that the man should stay out of the kitchen, and stop with the decorating already. Boy, have we gone off the mark.

Riddle----- Q-What is the difference between a man that is a chef in a restaurant, and a man that cooks at home?

A- One is working and is in a provider capacity, the other is in a nurturing capacity, which is not a masculine energy.

Riddle----- Q-What is the difference between a married man that is a decorator at work, and a married man that takes the role of decorator in the home?

A-Did you get it? One is making a living taking care of his family. The other, is a man that has overridden his wife's energy and has now become the nest builder. Of course, most men don't really want to decorate, but they are learning to as boys, and as they do, it seems their masculine energy is getting weaker.

Men, stay out of the feminine energy. Doing that will automatically push the woman into her natural role. Many women are insecure about cooking today, because they've had no role models as little girls. Men don't fall into the trap of taking over. Tell her how terrific she is with her cooking, and eventually she will want to go into the kitchen, and she will enjoy cooking as long as the male doesn't tear her down. Women love their kitchens and they really don't want the man in there unless they need the male's help once in a while. Men, remember you are the providers. Don't drain your energy on her roles. It seems great at first, but it will eventually kill the relationship. She will lose respect for herself and you.

<u>Remember she is always testing you to make sure you are a man, strong enough to take care of her and her family, as a provider/protector.</u>

Women, make sure he uses the screwdriver and hammer. I know you know how to use them. Let him change the license plate, and put up the shelves. Always keep him in his masculine energy.

If we start to reverse these insignificant things, we will start doing more and more automatically. Eventually we will both get frustrated as the energy circle starts to get out of balance, and a role reversal starts to occur.

Why should a woman never work for money, except in a supportive role? Because it takes her out of her feminine energy. She gradually becomes a provider, acting and thinking like a man. Those of you that are reading this, in many cases, know what I'm talking about. Of course, if you are single, you have to fill in the opposite energy. If and when you enter into a serious relationship the opposite energy slowly has to be released. Don't be afraid; your life will be a lot better for it. <u>The masculine energy for a woman is survival, and feminine energy for a man is survival.</u>

Coming from our own birthright energy, whether masculine or feminine, is a much happier experience.

SEE GOD IN WOMAN, ADORE HER AS THE ENERGY ASPECT OF THE LORD

Swami Sivananda

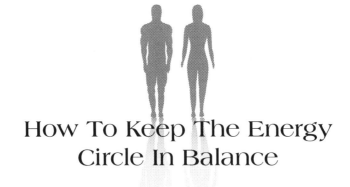

How To Keep The Energy Circle In Balance

Show love always.

Be respectful always.

Care about the other person's feelings always.

Give yourself time to communicate with each other, your feelings, thoughts, happiness and whenever they occur, your tears.

Listen to the other person without judging.

Only use positive words. (If you have nothing nice to say, why say anything at all?)

Share some heathy spiritual time daily.

Keep <u>live plants and flowers</u> in the house, as they uplift the energy.

Do not infringe on the other person's roles, except to temporarily help out, or in emergency situations.

Hugging is very important, and lots of it.

Give a gift to express love. The gift should come from your heart.

Never take your relationship for granted

******* Plus other nice, wonderful things you might think of.*******

How The Energy Circle Is Kept In Balance By Role Playing

MASCULINE ENERGY
provider-protector(enfolder)

Provide for the family
financially.

Be the physical strength
of the family.
       (she needs that)

Remember to give her live
flowers. Buy her feminine
gifts. A stuffed animal.
for the little girl inside.

Take her out for a
romantic dinner.

Remember to tell her
how pretty she is, and
how much she is loved.

Always be a gentleman.
Those manners keep her
in her feminine energy.

Be the protector of your mate.

FEMININE ENERGY
nurturer-nest bidder

Keep a nice home.

Cook homemade meals.

       (he needs that)

Rub his shoulders and
neck once in a while.

Make him feel like a man. He
needs your wonderful, supportive,
nurturing help and love.

Buy him presents, masculine in
nature, certainly not a pink shirt
unless you want to soften him up.

Keep thinking of more ideas along these lines that will keep the balance of the circle. Soon you will understand the concept. It gets easier as you go along.

WHAT OTHER IDEAS CAN YOU THINK OF?

Love

There is no difficulty that enough love will not conquer; No disease that enough love will not heal; No door that enough love will not open; No gulf that enough love will not bridge; No wall that enough love will not throw down; No sin that enough love will not redeem.

It makes no difference how deeply seated may be the trouble, How hopeless the outlook, How muddled the tangle, How great the mistake; A sufficient realization of love will dissolve it all. If only you could love enough you would be the happiest and most powerful being in the world.

Emmit Fox

Two Pieces

Long before I ever thought about the contents that I'm writing here, I wrote these two pieces about my childhood, and my parents. My parents were married 66 years. As an adult, these are my feelings and memories about them. If I didn't put these pieces in this book, I feel my book would be incomplete, as my parents made a major impact on shaping my life.

My mother passed away at almost ninety one; my father is still alive at ninety five. It was my sister and me, all the grandchildren and great grandchildren that got my father over the hurdle of my mother's death, so that he could keep going. The love you give you definitely get back. They set a wonderful example of how to be married and how to love their children. I didn't say they were perfect as parents, but I certainly wouldn't want any others.

I Am Special

My mother used to hold me in her wonderful lap and cuddle me. She would hum a lullaby and rock me to sleep, making the troubles of my little world disappear.

I was always tucked into bed and kissed good night. I felt loved and went to sleep with good feelings, knowing that my mother really cared.

My mother would share special times with me and make me feel important. She would sacrifice some of her own needs and give instead to me. She shared a lot of her personal life, so that I could understand what I was all about.

I had many questions about myself when I was young and she was always there to answer them.

Her answers were honest; she always made me feel good. I remember those wonderful talks we used to have.

Her heart was so good, her love so strong.

My mother had a lot of pain inside her.

I saw my mother cry a few times. I wished I had seen her cry more.

My mother was very bright. Why did it take me so long to know?

She gave from her heart, and anyone she came in contact with felt very special.

Her heart is solid gold. I love my mother, her strengths, her weaknesses, her kindness.

I will always be her little boy. She is still always there to kiss and hug me. We still share those great talks.

As an adult, I cherish all that she is and love to remember my childhood with her. I no longer take her for granted, or the wonderful love that she gave to me.

I think about her a lot. I've been blessed and I know it. My heart is my mother's, I am special.

I Can Remember

He didn't smile very much. Oh, how I loved to see him laugh. That was very important to me, to see him happy, it made me able to take all his gaff.

He loved his family very much. He would show that every day.

I can remember, in the past, we seemed rich, and then the bills were hard to pay.

My father was very bright, too bright, success was again difficult to obtain.

With all the stuff that went on at home, I can remember there was some pain.

But, ya know, I wouldn't change it for the world, all the same.

Life was so great when I was a kid, I felt I had it all. The inadequacies went by unnoticed, they were unimportant, and they would fall.

Eddie Cantor, Jimmy Durante, Jack Benny, they seemed to make my father's day. It's a shame those people are gone, I'd get them back in a minute, if I could have my way.

Baseball was the big sport when I was a boy, my father taught me how to play. I am lefty, he'd switch hands, and he would also throw that way.

My dad spent a lot of time with me when I was growing up. He taught me so much of what I know today, there's very little that I lack. I know that If I were in a jam, he'd give me the shirt right off his back.

He wasn't perfect. He made a lot of mistakes in his life, but the love for his family was his perfection, his success, it seemed to wash out all his strife.

Sometimes, I look in the mirror. I stand there in amazement.

I have my father's feet, his voice, and sometimes when I look real hard, I can see him smile. Then, all of a sudden, out comes his wonderful laugh, and then I know for certain I am his child.

Set a positive example for your children as best you can. That example will help them to have a happy adult life.

What Goes Into The Mind Is Recreated By The Mind

Thought Creates Form

What we believe is real, becomes real. What enters the mind, if repeated enough times, those impressions will create our reality. If we see or hear anything over and over again, we will probably carry out that reality in our own life. This is not a new idea as society would have us believe. This has been known for thousands of years. Hear or see negative information and we will live by that information. The younger we are when the negative message occurs, the more difficult it is to correct. Hear and see positive, happy information, from a young age and we will live by that information.

If one doesn't conquer their fears, there's a good chance they will pass some or all of their fears onto their children, just like their parents passed their fears onto them.

The following story I hope you will appreciate and enjoy. It will change your life if you understand and use the concept.

The following is an example of how Thought Creates Form

If people give by deeds, and words positive information, people of all ages will respond in a positive way. If a thought is negative, don't say it; if a deed is negative, don't do it.

<u>KINDNESS IS ACTION OF THOUGHT, WORD, AND DEED.</u>

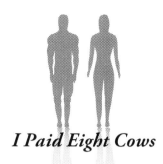

I Paid Eight Cows

Our story takes place in a third world country on an island. Our hero's name is Johnny. Johnny wants to get married. On the island, Johnny is highly respected. He's a tour guide, earns a lot of money, knows a lot of people, and is considered to be smart. He wants to get married, so he approaches his friend for some advice. On this island, if a man wants to get married, he has to give the father a gift for his bride to be; in this country it's cows. Cows are a sign of worth, so Johnny says to his friend, "I would like to marry this girl, how many cows should I give the father?"

His friend wants to know why Johnny would ever want to marry her. His reasons: she's not smart, pretty, never smiles, doesn't take care of herself, and just about every negative thing you could say about one person. "She's absolutely a nothing of a person, why would you ever want to marry her?" "Because I love her," Johnny says. "Well then, give the father one cow, that's all she's worth, but if he won't go for one, maybe two or three, but no more, because you know the beautiful women on this island get five cows given for them."

Johnny went home to think about what his friend had said. He paced the floor all night. Early in the morning Johnny came to a decision, got showered and shaved, got himself dressed and went to see the girl's father. "I would like to marry your daughter," Johnny said. "I will give you eight cows for her hand in marriage." Well the father was delighted beyond belief. The father would become rich with eight cows and get rid of this nothing of a person to boot. "Take my daughter, get her out of here as fast as you can," said the father. Johnny and his new wife left for Johnny's house.

Everyone in town heard the story. Johnny was the laughing stock of the island. Johnny had made a terrible mistake. Maybe he had gone mad, or wasn't smart after all. The people had lost respect for Johnny.

In comes a tourist who wants to see the island. The tourist stops a man and asks him if someone could show him around the island. He's told about Johnny, but also about his incredible mistake, and that people no longer believed much in Johnny. "Well, then I must see Johnny," he said to the man, "since there's no one else to show me around." The man pointed in the direction of Johnny's house on the remote section of the island. No one had seen Johnny, or his wife, for about six months.

The tourist finally met up with Johnny. They started to negotiate the price of seeing the island and up walked a woman. She was bringing them drinks. She was beautiful, absolutely gorgeous. She had a glow, a beautiful smile, her posture was perfect, her look was magnificent. Her eyes sparkled full of life. She just had it all.

"Who is that," asked the tourist? "That's my wife," said Johnny. "Wait a minute, how could this be your wife? I was told she was a nothing of a person. This may be the most magnificent woman I have ever seen," said the tourist. "How is this possible?" "Well," said Johnny, "If I had paid one, two, or three cows for her, she would have been a loser and she would have known it. If I had given five cows for her, she would have been just another pretty face. I paid eight cows for her, she is the most magnificent woman on this island and she knows it."

The above story has changed so many lives that I thank its author, whomever he or she is, a million times over.

THOUGHT CREATES FORM. WHAT THE MIND BELIEVES, IT CREATES.

Law Of The Universe

Put out love and it will come back many times over.

Put out praise and its rewards will be beyond belief.

Put out positive thoughts and people will become wonderful.

Give money generously.

What is put out is received many times over.

****

What is the solution to get the greatest power from people, a creation of God. To define more correctly, we are all God.

BUILD SELF ESTEEM.

ALLOW PEOPLE TO EXPRESS FREELY.

SEND MESSAGES OF LOVE ALWAYS.

CREATE A HEALTHY ENVIRONMENT.
(live flowers help to remove negative energy)

**(EXPAND OUT ALWAYS - TO CONTRACT
IS TO WHITHER AWAY)**

**_THE CREATIVE GENIUS OF MAN IS
UNLIMITED WHEN NOURISHED._**

A piece received by me at about 4am in the morning. It came through the
air and into my head. I immediately wrote it down.

How To Handle A Woman

"How to handle a woman?
There's a way," said the wise old man,
"A way known by every woman
Since the whole rigamarole began."

"Do I flatter her?" I begged him answer.
"Do I threaten or cajole or plead?
Do I brood or play the gay romancer?"
Said he smiling, "No, indeed."

written by
Lerner and Loewe,
from *Camelot*

There is only one answer. The answer is for EVERYONE.
The answer is the word **LOVE!**

Some More One-Liners

Don't be in a rut, be in a marriage.

What does it behoove a man or woman to gain the world and lose his or her soul?

Women infuse the religious spirit in men through their daily conduct.

Without a woman, the home is void; without her, the man is helpless; without her the world loses all charm; without her, there is no creation. She controls the destiny of the children. She silently rules and governs the world.

Marriage is a sacred union of soul with soul.

Wolves mate for life.

Effort creates change.

Love in time of stress is a healing, a centering.

To hold anger, closes down the heart. It creates disease, unhappiness, and prevents true personal growth.

Change your thoughts and you change your world.

Love is not a state of mind, it just is.

Is your marriage a script of your parents, or is your marriage from your heart?

The Sun is always shining.
The Clouds that block the Sun
will one day move away.
The Sun will shine again.

YOU'RE NEVER UPSET FOR THE REASON YOU THINK
YOU'RE NEVER UPSET FOR THE REASON YOU THINK

It Doesn't Belong There

Our body is like a magnet. It pulls into it all kinds of things that don't belong there. I call these things <u>negative energy</u>. Ya know, things like stress, dis-ease, and anger. If we don't forgive someone, we hold onto that negative energy. If we swallow our feelings, that goes into our body also. The energy can appear to the naked eye as a tightness. Our neck and shoulders don't feel free. Our hands might appear clenched, our arms might be folded, or our face might appear contorted. We may get headaches or illnesses. If we play sports, or work out with weights, we pull in energy that appears to make us larger. Our body may be slowly contracting to eventually create an injury, or explosion, actually springing out of control.

When the body is getting pumped up with contracted energy, that energy has to come out somewhere. On the playing field, the game of football requires the player to have a lot of energy built up in order to hit hard, but we are doing the same thing off the field. People, both men and women, are screaming at one another, hitting one another, hurting one another, because they are not in balance. They are loaded with negative energy, and in so many cases we are taking it out on the ones we love most.

If you have that negative energy in you, get rid of it. Get a massage, take a yoga class, go to see a therapist, get out in nature, go for a long walk, or listen to peaceful music. Go to a place of worship, read a spiritual book, and pray. Don't take it out on your wife, or husband, or children, or friends, or relatives. If necessary, go into a private room and beat up a pillow, or scream as loud as you can, or cry, cry, cry! Get rid of that negative energy at all costs, without hurting someone else, or yourself. So many people are hurting one another, and, I know, five minutes later they wish they hadn't.

Free Choice

This planet came into existence billions of years ago. Everything was set up to work in perfect harmony. There was a blueprint of sorts, and everything worked with it. There was a perfect balance in nature. The sun came up every day, four seasons per year, a full moon, and then a new moon. There was definitely a circle of life with all of nature, including all of God's creatures. Life always moved according to a preplanned program, and then mankind was put on this planet.

Remember, everything out there has intelligence, but it's more instinctive. Then all of a sudden something new was put on this earth - **us**. We too, were very connected to the earth. We were a part of the earth and we knew that. There was something different about us though. Something that would set us apart from all of nature. Something that could make, or break the balance of the world. The human being alone could do that. That something is called FREE CHOICE.

Mankind can actually do what it wants. If humanity wants to destroy the air, soil, trees, water, animals, or anything, it can. Free choice is so incredible, because we have the right to do anything we want, good or bad, and anything in between. But there are tremendous consequences to it if we misuse the free choice that we are given. We can destroy everything around us, and can even destroy ourselves. It's like what goes around comes around, and what you give, you get back, and generally more than you gave. The Yogis call it Karma.

Of course, the above would be another book, if it weren't for the fact that men and women, too, are preprogrammed to live out their lives happily, again a blueprint that we have literally torn apart by free choice. It is my belief that the sole purpose of religion was and is to keep that blueprint working properly, to keep us centered, in balance, and in harmony with this entire universal experience.

Of course, the leaders of religion had free choice too, so it got manipulated, but not the original ideas. The original religious teachings came from very highly evolved souls, who were trying to lead us to the Truth. They were spiritual people, more evolved, their teachings all being very much alike. You know what they are: love one another, treat each other well, respect one another, love your family, etc. We've all been blessed with The Ten Commandments, The Sermon On The Mount, the teachings on forgiveness, the universal prayer, singing and chanting to create positive thoughts, and to serve, love, and give to this planet and everything that encompasses it.

It is only the human being that can override the instinctive blueprint. With free choice created through our ego, our computer brain, we can do anything we want. Just as thoughts can be placed into a home computer, we can do the same to our brain, going against our instinctive birthright roles. If you want to do it, you can; of course, that doesn't mean you'll be happy. That's what people are doing nowadays. Men are becoming women, women are becoming men, and we're getting everything in between, all for power, materialism, and ego. We can see the society suffering because of it. Let's stop divorce, stop verbal and physical abuse, stop prejudice, and stop hatred.

That's what the spiritual leaders were trying to get us to do. Get us in sync, back to real values, back to the truth, back to the way that we all can live happily.

DID YOU KNOW THAT GEESE MATE FOR LIFE?
(what a nice instinct to have.)

Divorce

If you take the plunge, and make the commitment to get married, then as the marriage vows state, it's until death do you part. All religions, somewhere in their teachings, talk about marriage as a lifetime commitment. They have material that one can read, they have counseling, and they go to great lengths to try and prevent a divorce from occurring. To my knowledge, the religion that takes divorce the most seriously is CATHOLICISM. The Catholic Church doesn't just try and prevent a divorce from happening, it says ABSOLUTELY NOT, NO WAY, NOT AT ALL; divorce is not allowed. You know what? They were, and are, absolutely correct. Against all kinds of pressure, the leadership of the Catholic Church has stuck to the teachings, to the laws, and to the rules.

The great thinkers, who set up the written law, had a tremendous amount of foresight and wisdom. They knew that once divorce was in society, it would run rampant, like a cancerous growth, and would, over time, have a great negative power to destroy everything in its path. The great seers, in those days, knew also, that once in a while a marriage was wrong and could not be saved. There was no hope. There was absolutely no way that the marriage could work, and I'm sure with great deliberation and thorough investigation a decision of separation was finally decided upon and issued. The document that was issued was called an annulment. It was not even closely considered to be a divorce. The annulment was the last resort to prevent serious destruction to the family. The split was permitted. In this rare case, a short circuit of monumental proportions was taking place during the marriage. Usually the most extreme short circuit takes place after the separation. This is why divorce is such a tragedy.

IF MARRIED COUPLES COULD UNDERSTAND THAT MOST
OF THE TIME DIVORCE WOULD <u>NOT</u> BE A STEP FORWARD,
BUT GENERALLY A STEP SIDEWAYS OR BACKWARDS, THEY
MIGHT TAKE A SECOND LOOK.

The divorce rate is over 50% in the United States, and in some areas of
the U.S. climbing towards 60%. We are being misled by the media, and
by people who are divorced, and don't tell the truth about their lives. We
believe they're happy, and so we want to be just like them. In fact, in many,
many cases, they're miserable, but don't want anyone else to know. We've
become such a selfish society, that we only think of ourselves. We are so
disconnected from the truth, so out of touch with reality, that we can't see
the writing in front of our nose. We are so desensitized, that we actually
think divorce will make us happy. As the statistics show, nothing could
be further from the truth.

Most divorces just don't solve the long term problem. They don't give the
person, or persons, the happiness that they are trying to achieve. On a short
term basis, they seem to work. We have a new freedom, a feeling of I can
do with my life what I want to. But, as the mind now gets used to that
feeling, the true reality of divorce starts to set in. Although most divorced
people tell their friends of their highs, they forget to tell them about their
lows. When people get divorced, they say with frustration or anger, I don't
want to be with the opposite sex, I can do just fine by myself. That seems
to be only temporary, and the need to complete the circle of energy, again
begins to take place. The need to be in contact with the opposite energy
of either masculine or feminine, again occurs. Yes, yes I know that we're
being told that we should be able to be self-contained with both energies,
but my belief is that only a few on this planet have been able to do this
successfully. Without the opposite energy of either masculine or feminine,
our immune system slowly weakens, many people go into depression and
many die earlier than they should. It's been proven that hugs and touches
and love keep us happy and very much alive.

When we live alone we can go off balance and short circuit. So, we are
constantly looking for a mate, or the disaster is, we give up and block

or turn off our feelings. I've witnessed depression, nervous breakdowns, immense loneliness, physical ailments, suicides, and early, so called, natural deaths. To try to keep in balance, people drink alcohol or take drugs. They go to doctors more often for problems that don't exist. They fill up their time with anything just to stay busy, like traveling a lot. In some cases single people actually become drifters. These things are amazing to me, but because we short circuit, we become completely out of balance, and are always struggling to get back to that balanced, centered feeling; you know, the one that puts a smile back on our face. So, marriage absolutely works, and for most, divorce does not.

If a couple has children, the problems are even more difficult, and more serious. Whatever makes us think that we can ever get rid of that spouse? That person will alway be a part of their own original family energy circle, connected together, as long as they or their children are alive. It's our personal energy circle, never to dissolve except upon death. So what's been gained? Nothing!!!! So, if we have children, it becomes even more complicated.

Women, generally getting custody of their children, nowadays, have two full time jobs. One is to be the mother, taking care of the home and the children. The other is to play father, and the man of the house. The mental and physical exhaustion and stress are incredible. On top of that, the woman eventually wants to date, meet someone special again, and generally wants to get married. How do you do that? It can be done, but it's a juggling act at best. And even if she gets married, the new husband will never be a part of the energy circle with the child, and he will probably want a child of his own, if he's young enough. So now there are two children, and two different energy circles. It's a tough time had by all.

The man has it just as bad. He generally loses much of the enjoyment and support of his family, but still has the responsibility of paying child support and alimony, while trying to keep his head on straight for his job. He, also, would like to meet someone, and get married, but can he afford it? If he does get married, he also, will have two energy circles, and his new wife, if young enough, will probably want kids. What a mess for all. And who pays, most of all, for this lunatic, immature, behavior of the parents? You guessed it, the children. Now really, what a mess! Sometimes the man fades out, even though he tries not to, and loses the ability to earn money. He no longer can maintain the mental balance to take care of his family without the wife's feminine energy for support. If married again, taking care of two families may be just too much.

The children, as hard as they try, love their own parents more, and the adults, as hard as they try, love their own children more.

Why So Much Pain? Why Does It Hurt So Much When A Divorce Occurs?

Remember the two candles, those lights merging into one light? That's exactly what happens to the two adults that get married. Slowly, during their courting, if the two of them finally reached a point of being in sync with each other, they were now ready to get married. During the first year or so of marriage, the rest of the kinks were usually worked out. Our bodies and minds started to fuse, or merge together, our cells becoming as one, just like the flame. That doesn't mean that we don't exist independently, but we certainly become fused together as one, as well. Many times we see people that even look alike, and certainly begin to know what the other person is going to say before they say it. Sometimes, the inflection in their voices sounds the same, even if they came from different parts of the country, or world.

If the above is true, then it is understandable that a divorce would play tremendous havoc on each partner. A marriage, as discussed before, is a completed energy circle, and like the flame, a combining of two human beings melded into one. Is it any wonder what happens during and after the divorce; it's total craziness, total pain. Every cell of the body is torn apart and separated. This takes years for the complete separation, if it happens at all. The brain goes through even more hell. Remember, it gradually fused together as if being slowly welded. Now the brain is being torn, ripped apart, or shredded. It's no wonder people do destructive things to each other, the pain is so severe. It takes years for the pain to go away if it ever goes away at all. The pain gets less, but it may never go completely away, because of the energy circle that exists, which will never fully disappear between the two partners and their children, and because of the powerful impressions in the mind, that cannot be erased.

Can you imagine how the children feel if this is what the parents are going through? The children are literally ripped in two. Their entire world is being torn apart. This will happen as long as the child is still a part of the energy circle. Even if the person has grown up and left the energy circle there will always be some permanent damage. The following are what I've noticed in my own life and from my own personal experiences talking to many people: so-called accidental death, serious and life threatening illnesses, obesity, tremendous anger and fear, and the inability to get married, copying divorce creating the reality again and again of their childhood experience. Also, alcoholism, use of drugs, committing crimes, women marrying much older men to recapture what they lost as children, boys having strong feminine energy because there was no man around to balance them out, children in therapy for the rest of their lives, because of their parents selfishness. Who in this world would want their child to go through this?

Deadbeat Dads

Did you know that today women are asking for over 60% of the divorces? Of course, they also want the kids, alimony, and child support. Why not, in this world, get as much as you can. We sure have great values, don't we? Get a divorce from a marriage that we're not happy in, and then try to get as much as we can for ourselves, even if we created 50% of the problem. We sure have learned to take responsibility for our lives, haven't we? I'm not saying everyone is doing this, but I'm sure it's happening more than we can even dream. So now we've created a mess. The man is sent on his way to find a new life, but he still has to take care of the old one.

Most men love their families. They would do anything in the world for them, but sometimes can't when there is no support system. Of course, everyone pays for a divorce in the end. Some people have problems with their kids; sometimes you see someone die prematurely; sometimes you see someone become a drug addict, or alcoholic; sometimes someone has a nervous breakdown, but of course these don't count. Remember, we belong to the "me" generation. What a laugh; selfish people looking out for themselves and pointing the finger at someone else, never taking responsibility for their own actions.

If a man has a strong support system, he can conquer the world. Without one, he may just fall in the mud and stay there. So he's called a deadbeat dad. Try keeping two roles and keeping your head on straight. If the man is divorced, he has to take care of his home, take responsibility in his job, make sure he sees his children, and still financially support his family. Thank God for the new woman who will put up with this guy. It's probably the only thing that keeps him close to sane. Hopefully he has immediate family, like parents, or brothers, or sisters, that will keep him sane as well. He should make sure he goes to religious services and sees a therapist as a form of support, if he can afford one. Of course, many men don't have some of those support systems, so they totally fall apart, and many, you guessed it, become deadbeat dads.

By the way, it's not so simple for the woman either. How many woman do you know, that without the males support, mentally lose it and become unable to take care of their family. Could we possibly call them deadbeat moms? Divorce just doesn't work.

****

AS THE FAMILY GOES, SO GOES THE NATION.

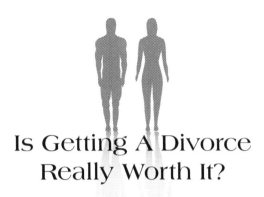

Is Getting A Divorce
Really Worth It?

What the marriage vows say is, WORK THROUGH YOUR PROBLEMS - GO FOR HELP- DON'T SCREW UP YOUR LIFE AND YOUR FAMILYS' LIFE. Don't buy into this destructive, cancerous negativity. If conventional methods of therapy won't work, try other means. Don't give up. DON'T GIVE UP! Your life, and your familys' life, is at stake. DIVORCE IS NOT THE SOLUTION.

**** If two people get married, and have no children, a divorce can be easier, because the energy circle begins to dissolve upon the divorce.****

THREE OF THE MOST COMMON REASONS FOR DIVORCE:

1. Immaturity - being too young emotionally to get married.
2. Not making a total commitment to the marriage.
3. Becoming a forest dweller, and not understanding that you are entering a new phase of your life. (A very high percentage of divorces occur at this time. You will read about the forest dweller stage in an upcoming chapter.)

I Want A Divorce

People are getting divorced, and in many cases, they don't even know why. We are all so programmed with the word, that we, in some cases, are on automatic pilot. Divorce is all around us. We hear about it on television, in the newspapers, and in tabloids. Songs write about it, and movies talk about it; divorce is just everywhere. If we are programmed with the message, we may carry it out and not even know why. We could create the reality that our brain has been programmed with. If our parents are divorced, divorce may occur because our brain is triggered to play a message that we might not want to act on, but we believe we're supposed to. It's possible that we will recreate our parents divorce, or someone else's reality, in our own personal life.

That's how the brain works. We believe we're supposed to carry out the reality of the triggered message, even if it's somebody else's message. The message is received through our senses. The impressions enter the mind and are recorded in our brain, just like a tape recorder. Eventually the message will play in the brain, and we may carry out whatever the tape plays, unaware that it is <u>not</u> our own creation. I'll bet many divorces happen only because the tape played out somebody else's experience, and what we thought was our reality, we carried out.

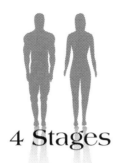

4 Stages

There are four stages of life, three of which we understand, and the fourth, which most of us are completely unaware of. Many divorces occur during this fourth stage of life. This information can become very heavy, so here's a funny piece on the four stages of life, just to make you laugh, or smile a little.

1. We believe in Santa Claus
2. We don't believe in Santa Claus
3. We act like Santa Claus
4. We look like Santa Claus

Did you laugh, just a little?

Now to the real four stages of life.

1. 1. Childhood
2. 2. Student
3. 3. Family
4. 4. Forest dweller

The fourth stage of life is a very interesting stage because it's so simple to understand, yet very few people ever discuss it. It's when the children are on the verge of, or have left the nest, or to put it another way, when the children are on the verge of leaving the couple's energy circle. It's when we believe our responsibilities are over as parents, and sometimes it's very premature. We can walk into the forest together, or we can walk in alone. We have a choice, and that choice many of us don't understand. Our society is not geared for being alone. We do not have a support system such as a small community to live in where people eat together and share responsibilities. The forest dweller stage is the final stage before we leave the planet to move on. We generally become more spiritual, more questioning, as we were in the early stages of childhood. If you take a look, you'll find that many divorces occur as this stage begins to unfold. One partner will probably go through the forest dweller stage earlier than the other. It's important to recognize this stage, and work through it together.

MARRIAGE IS UNTIL DEATH DO YOU PART.
Keep the Commitment

Forest Dweller

When one looks at all the women getting into politics, when one sees all the women being broadcasters in all areas of television, when one is clear enough to really see what is going on, all one can do is say "help" and cringe.

I hope everyone knows that we teach by example and the words we use. The forest dweller stage is a time when life begins to move to the next step. For the men, their responsibility is slowing down as provider. For the women, their role of mother is not needed as much.

So we again go forward in our lives. If women want to work in this stage, that's okay. If men want to work less, it's easy to understand. But, don't forget, we teach by example and the words we use. When the women, during World War II, went into the factories and into the military, they did these things to help our country stay free, not because they wanted to, but because they had to. They were defending their children and their grandchildren. It was a matter of survival, not to change the way we would function after the war. Women needed to come back into the homes again, and the men needed to come back to their families. Many did. These people put their families first, always!

When a person's life moves into the forest dweller stage, do they make sure that the younger generation knows what they did in the past? It's important for the young woman to know that the women that are now working in high profile positions, did not sacrifice their families for their own personal gain, greed or ego. That they were at home until they were no longer needed at home. That they were there for their families, and are still there even though a shift has taken place. It's important that the men let the next generation know that they were there for their families, as providers and protectors (enfolders), and are still there for their wives as providers and protectors (enfolders), and will always be there for their families, even though their role has somewhat changed.

We have to tell the next generation, somehow, that we were there for our families, otherwise they will only know what they see now and they will take for granted that these are the things we have always done. We have to stop what the younger generation now believes, that they should conquer the world, and then be there for their family. If we've made mistakes, we've got to own up to them. How else will the next generation learn? And when we do work we should work to make a positive difference in society, not for our own selfish good. At least I hope that's what we will do.

If the next generation knows the truth, then maybe they'll think twice about getting married and having children if they're not willing to make a full commitment to their families. Men need to work for money, not for wealth and power, but to take care of and love their families and to make a positive difference in this world. That should be their only reasons. Mothers, and wives need to be doing the same thing at home. If they are not, then we are all losing.

Centers Of Energy

There are seven main invisible energy centers in the human body. These subtle energy centers, called chakras, are closely related to the physical body, as well as emotionally, mentally and spiritually connected. One main energy center is located near the heart, and one is located near the genital area. They work something like this: when the female is sexually aroused, the sexual energy generally moves from the upper body, and works its way down to the lower energy center, or both centers will function simultaneously. When the male is sexually aroused, the lower center generally functions first; the love center may not react at all. That's why the woman usually thinks first on a sexual level, and the man will generally react first. Men usually think about sex first, and women generally think about love. Women have been trying to override their true nature and act like men, but it really hasn't worked. Men have tried to change too, but it hasn't really worked. We sure are opposites in so many ways.

Sometimes, a woman without even realizing it, gives off so much invisible sexual energy, that it can make a man crazy and he may do irrational things. Don't forget, men usually react first, and that gets men into a lot of trouble. A man, too, gives off sexual energy that no one can see, but the woman may think first before she reacts. Love, not sex, is generally her motivation.

In today's times, the sexual arousal levels are kept very high. Magazines, movies, and TV, are all working to keep the sexual energies working at peak performance. Since the man reacts first, and because the woman's sexual invisible energy is so, so powerful at certain times, I believe that many cultures used clothing in such a way as to shut down those sexual energies from coming through. It's certainly something to think about.

We can't always change the nature of the animal, but we certainly can do more to prevent the problem of the way the male animal reacts.

Questions

Is it possible that the Divine Mother and one or more of the invisible, upper energy centers (chakras), are one and the same? Is it possible that both the boy and the girl have the Divine Mother inside but at an early age that energy center closes down or partially closes down in the boy? Is it possible that the same energy centers that have shut down in the boy, are now closing down in the girl as she moves more towards the masculine energy? Is it possible that love, and proper exercise such as Yoga, and Tai Chi gradually open up these centers? Is it possible that the closer one gets to a vegetarian diet, the more the upper energy centers open? It is possible that prayer, chanting, spiritual singing, and positive phrases open the upper energy centers?

Is it possible that the Divine Mother and the upper energy centers, chakras, are one and the same?

Sex Can Destroy Your Marriage

The above is a pretty heavy, powerful statement. In today's world, we are being made to believe that everything revolves around sex. Well, first of all, it doesn't. Sex is important, but too much sex may actually be an energy drain especially for the male. Certainly, men don't think clearly, sometimes, when that vital energy leaves the body.

To me, intimacy is terrific. Cuddling, hugging, kissing, touching, and saying wonderful words are all very important for a relationship to work, but vital energy loss due to sexual excess, may create a separation, instead of bringing a couple together.

I'm sure everyone is aware that we all have energies coming from our being all the time. Some people can actually see our auras. They see different colors surrounding us. I've never really been able to see an aura. I have been able to feel sexual energy though, being transmitted from someone else. Sometimes, it's so strong, that it can almost blow a person over. Did you ever feel that kind of energy? I'll bet most of you have. It's part of what brings us together, and keeps us together. Of course don't be fooled by this energy. If there's no other substance, other than sexual energy, it would be pretty hard to keep a marriage working long term.

Sexual energy, pulling two people together, can be absolutely wonderful. It's so powerful, so exciting, but it dissipates with intercourse. Each time a couple has sex, one time after the other, after the other, in a short period of time, the sexual energy slowly diminishes, and eventually can be reduced to almost zero. Maybe that's when a fight occurs, and then we may make up when the sexual energy builds again. That just may be why we are pulled back together. It takes a few days for that energy to again build up. Is it possible when the sexual energy is gone, we think we don't love that person anymore? Is it possible that when that sexual energy gets weaker, that we sometimes think of getting out of our marriage? It's something to really think about. We may be fooling ourselves.

Don't get out of your marriage. Work through your problems. You'll be happy you did.

"Freedom is not the ability to do anything we want. Rather, freedom is the ability to live responsibly the truth of our relationship with God and with one another."

Pope John Paul II
Jan. 26, 1999 while in the U.S.

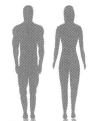

The Ten Commandments

I AM THE LORD YOUR GOD, YOU SHALL HAVE NO OTHER GODS BEFORE ME.

YOU SHALL NOT MAKE FOR YOURSELF AN IDOL IMAGE.

REMEMBER THE SABBATH DAY, TO KEEP IT HOLY.
(Take one day a week, any day, and make that one day a week a special day, and please, spend time with your family.)

YOU MUST NOT TAKE THE NAME OF THE LORD YOUR GOD IN VAIN.
(Please stop all the swearing, and again, please don't use the word God in vain.)

HONOR YOUR FATHER AND YOUR MOTHER.
(This has two meanings: honor your Father God, and your Mother Earth, and be good to your parents, honor them.)

YOU MUST NOT KILL. You must not use physical or verbal abuse.

YOU MUST NOT STEAL.

YOU MUST NOT LIE.

YOU MUST NOT COMMIT ADULTERY.

YOU MUST NOT ENVY.

These laws of the universe were set down to make each one of our lives better, yet in many cases we have removed ourselves from practicing some, or all of them. If we practice and teach these laws, future generations will do the same and most of the difficulties that mankind has will be eliminated. These commandments should be repeated daily.

THOUGHTS DECIDE THE FUTURE and THOUGHT CREATES FORM. REMEMBER, WHAT GOES INTO THE BRAIN, AND IS REPEATED OVER AND OVER, WILL BE RECREATED BY THE BRAIN.

Are You Listening?

Today is March 9th, 1999. If I didn't write this piece today, I would probably be saying to myself forever, "Self, how come you didn't write about a great example of why we all should follow The Ten Commandments?" Examples are always being put out there of why one should not test them, but for some reason, people always feel they know better. The Ten Commandments are just too solid, too pure, too perfect, to have been written from the thoughts of man. In my life I've tested many of them, and my going against them has sure come back to haunt me. Sometimes, God gets so sick and tired of us going against his laws, that he puts some giant, monumental example out in front of us, so maybe we'll learn a great lesson from someone else's stuff.

He's probably saying, "Is anybody out there listening? Do I have to put more and more examples out there? Are you all so lost, so disconnected from the truth, that none of this means anything? I gave the world a real biggy, like AIDS, to stop sexual promiscuity. Some are listening, but not enough. I gave you some of the biggest names in sports to show violence between men and women, and you didn't get it. In fact, I gave you one of the biggest names in sports and entertainment that I could think of, and you made a television epic out of it. People made fortunes from it, selling books, etc. Is anybody out there listening?

Again, I've given you a really big one. I gave you the President of the United States and an unknown woman. How much higher up do I have to go. How much more of a mess do I have to create, to get the world to listen? I gave you the top political person in the world, and you laughed me off. Oh, not all of you, but way, way too many.

Here's what you've done with this most recent experience I've put before you, nothing worth while. Adultery destroys families, people, and lives. It may not look like it does, but it does. The media has made a joke of it, that's including TV, the news and magazines. I feel bad about that, because you haven't seen the worst of it. Adultery destroys. Why, otherwise, would I ever have made a commandment out of it? THOU MUST NOT COMMIT ADULTERY....period, period, period, no ands, ifs, or buts. In adultery there are no winners. Follow this story long enough and you'll see that, just like everything else that I've put out there before you. THOU MUST NOT LIE. No one can go against that commandment either, or it will eventually come back to haunt you many times over. I've tried to show that too, and you didn't go for it. You actually turned two of my Ten Commandments into a sham, as if they were just a bunch of words. You've taken my work, and you've said it's not important. You've taken a young woman who has extremely low moral values, and you've put her on a pedestal. You've made a hero out of her. All around the world she's known, instead of not known at all. You're snubbing one of the most important pieces I've ever sent down to earth, The Ten Commandments.

These examples were set to stop the abuse of so many, not to increase it. You don't understand that by making an example of this around the world, in homes, in churches, and in schools, that you are setting a trend for generations to come. Remember, I've set up the brain to work by impressions (samskaras). If the brain is recording negative information over and over again, that is how the person will carry out his or her life. What has happened, is that such a huge negative programming has taken place, especially on the young, that unless something stronger is done, the next generation is going to have a much tougher time. How far do I want to go? I'm not sure at this point. It all depends on you. My laws have already been written. All I ask people to do, is follow them."

The warriors I talk about in this chapter are of the lowest caliber. In fact they are not warriors at all, but destroyers. Please do not put them on a pedestal. The woman, I hope, will truly be remembered for what she really is. Please, teach your children these are not the paths to follow. (Because the negative programming has been so powerful, due to constant repetition by the media and idle gossip, the positive must be repeated over and over and over, hopefully, overriding the negative messages, now in many a mind.)

ONE MONTH AFTER THIS PIECE WAS WRITTEN,

LITTLETON, COLORADO OCCURRED.

WHAT'S NEXT?

THE LIST GOES ON AND ON AND ON
and will continue unless we learn to play the
game of life according to the rules.

ARE YOU LISTENING?

Reflections

So many times I hear people say: he or she treats me this way; they do this to me, or that to me; or I wish we could communicate more. Like I said in another chapter, we are fifty percent of the problem, and we seem to not want to take responsibility for our actions. We should treat each other with love and respect. If we did, that's exactly what would come back. If we didn't give up and treated the other person nicely, that's eventually how they would treat us. What we get is a reflection of ourselves. It take years to understand that. What you put out, you get back many times over. What goes around, comes around. That's the way it works. We get what we give.

Sometimes, I see children in therapy. All they are is a reflection of the adults around them. It shouldn't be the child in therapy, it should be the parents. Will we ever take the responsibility for kids being out of sync? When will we quit blaming the other person and look at ourselves instead?

****

If you grow a healthy tree, you'll pick healthy fruit. If you grow a diseased tree, you'll pick worm-eaten fruit. The fruit tells you about the tree.

Matthew 12:23:37

EVERY ACTION, CREATES A REACTION.

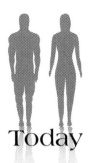

Today

Today, men talk to women as if they are men. Women act like that's how they would like to be treated. What we are being made to believe is a nontruth. A woman still wants to be treated like a woman. What a bunch of mixed signals we're all giving and getting. The roles are completely confused, and because of that, so are we, and so are our children. Instead of functioning from Love and Truth, we function from ego.

THE ONLY WAY TO TREAT ONE ANOTHER
IS WITH LOVE

Forgive And Go On

Most of us have never learned to forgive, and yet it is one of the major teachings of spirituality. Without forgiving someone, it's pretty hard to go forward. We hold in so much negative energy that way. By forgiving, we release a lot of the pain and hurt we feel inside. Forgiving is a way to heal oneself. I didn't say one had to be a weak person, and I didn't say we had to forget, but to let go and forgive will make your life a lot happier. A relationship will never work without forgiveness.

LET HE OR SHE THAT HAS NOT SINNED
CAST THE FIRST STONE
Do you really think anyone is going to throw that stone?

****

FORGIVENESS FREES THE HEART.
FORGIVENESS OPENS THE HEART
TO LOVE, TO GIVE, TO RECEIVE
FORGIVENESS IS A HEALING

Further Explanation Of
The Energy Circle

The energy circle is formed gradually with the relationship. Once a marriage has been completed, the circle is now formed. As the marriage continues, the circle gets stronger. (If there are no children, the circle will gradually dissolve if the marriage, or relationship, ends. The pain continues on, but the circle will slowly disappear.)

Having children is entirely different. When children become a part of the circle and a split occurs, the circle does not dissolve. It will exist until one of the adults passes away. Don't ever think that getting a divorce and trying to find another mate will be easy. You will always have the original circle as you are trying to form another one with a new mate. That new mate may want to strengthen their new circle by having a child of their own. You can see how difficult and complicated life can become. <u>It is not worth getting a divorce; work out your problems, get some good help, and don't give up.</u>

This book is for people who want a relationship and want to make it work forever. If you've never been married, and don't want to get married, understand that you are still setting an example for future generations. Also, an energy circle of sorts will have to be completed somehow, generally by a closer relationship with family, and spending more time with God, to keep you in balance, and to stay sane.

*Whether in a relationship, married, or single, God
is the most important grounding of all.*

*LOVE EACH OTHER
FOR YOUR DIFFERENCES, AS WELL AS YOUR SIMILARITIES*

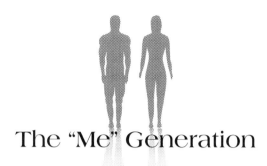

The "Me" Generation

Years ago I walked into a therapist's office for my own personal appointment. As I sat there, next to me was a woman with her young daughter. I knew both of them. I thought the woman was there for a session, and she needed, for lack of a sitter, to bring her daughter with her. I was wrong. The child was there because she needed help coping with her parent's divorce. I really hurt inside for that kid. As I sat there I got angrier and angrier. The parents got a divorce, and the child's in therapy! What are we doing? If we don't care about our own lives, don't we at least care about our kids lives? Are we that selfish? Aren't we aware that many times we're destroying our children by getting a divorce? Is it that our lives are the only ones that count? I sat there with so much emotion inside of me. Selfish people, thinking only of themselves. That's how we live our lives. We're called the "me" generation. We don't care about anyone else; we live for today. Doesn't tomorrow count as well?

When are we going to realize, that when our children hurt, we also feel the pain? In fact, we hurt more. When are we going to stop only thinking of ourselves? When are we going to grow up and get help for ourselves, so that our kids won't grow up, screwed up, like their parents?

A marriage is until death do you part. Make your marriage work. Don't be so immature as to destroy your life, and everybody else's too. Go to spiritual services. Consult good spiritual leaders. Read the Bible, and other books that help move you forward in a positive way. Don't feed into the negative. Live your life on the plus side. Divorce is a disaster for anyone, but even more so when you have kids. *The energy circle never dissolves, NEVER, when there are children.

****

*An adult death somewhat permits for the half of the energy circle to dissolve, allowing the circle to be completed again with a new mate. It still isn't easy, but the children should have an easier time adjusting.

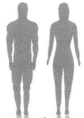

The Mating, Dating Again Ritual

Again, I may be repeating myself but, it's important to write that in many relationships and marriages nowadays, the woman gradually takes over the strong energy (masculine energy), and the man will, to fill the void, go over to the so-called weak side. Like I've stated, this out of balance circle will usually cause a major crack in the relationship. What's so interesting is, if a break up occurs, eventually we will want to meet someone again. When that happens, the woman will automatically exude that strong feminine energy to attract a mate, and the male will notably appear stronger in his masculine energy to also attract a mate. Some of the things we do are exercise, lose weight, and eat better. We may even buy some new clothes, so as to reinforce our masculine or feminine look. Why don't we help each other do this while we're in a relationship or marriage, so that a break up does not occur? If we communicate with each other, and take a good look at ourselves in the mirror, maybe we can.

Impressions

Did you ever hear of the word samskaras? You probably won't find the word in your home dictionary. It's a Sanskrit word coming from the oldest living language. The word and language come from India. It means impressions in the mind.

Did you know that thoughts decide the future, and that thought creates form? Did you know, that what is put into the brain, if repeated enough times, will eventually be recreated by the brain, and the body may act it out?

We're actually living our lives on how we are programmed, just like the computer on your desk or in your office. You're not really living your life from today's information, you're living your life from yesterday's. You, in many cases, are functioning from old information.

Have the brain record killing enough times and you may kill. If the brain records hate, prejudice, and anger, you probably will live that way. As the samskaras become stronger, we live on that script. If the brain records love, and happiness, and good role models, then that's the way you'll live your life. If you want to know what a person will be like, check out their parents. That's probably the strongest influence in their life. If the brain is programmed with divorce, you may get a divorce and not even know why. If we are aware that these tapes exist, then we have a chance to override the negative tapes with more positive information.

That is part of the function of religion, and the teachings of the great spiritual masters. Read, see, hear and feel positive thoughts each day from an early age on, and you'll live out a positive life. It's just as automatic as that.

That's what The Ten Commandments are all about. A program of good messages, if repeated daily, will help to make your life much happier. Reading the Bible, the Koran, the Bagavad Gita, and many other teachings daily help to program your mind and keep you functioning in a balanced, positive way. Going to religious services once or twice a day, does the same thing providing you have good spiritual leaders. Keep your wedding invitation out where you can see it. Keep the marriage vows out and read them. Put your wedding album out where it can be easily seen, and you won't get a divorce. The brain will recall how happy you were, the vows tell you until death do you part. Live out the program for positive living, correct your problems, and love your life.

I Love My Family

The mind learns from repetition. I make no excuses for repeating myself. In this book I've put phrases, here and there, but, I wanted to write a little more on the following. We're just plain being misled on many, many, issues. It's amazing to me that so many of us are so out of touch, that we're letting money and power control our lives. That we are not using our common sense to do the right thing. We must be so disconnected from the Truth within, that we are overriding right with wrong, and you know what, our gut must hurt a lot.

When a family breaks up, or a mother works, or a father doesn't pay attention to his kids, it can become a mess for the rest of their lives. Don't let anybody fool you, <u>love is all that works.</u> Not tough love, but balanced, centered, love. In order to turn a child into a good adult you can never give up on that child. Adults have to keep a child on a narrow path with true love, if not they could fall off on either side. We are their teachers. We have to keep ourselves as balanced and as centered as possible. That is what a woman does for a man, and vice versa. That's what a mother does for a daughter, and that's what a father does for a daughter. That's what a mother does for a son, and a father does for a son. Don't fall into the trap of thinking that your children will grow up mentally healthy on their own. Don't fall into the trap of believing that someone else could ever raise your child better than you can. Love, love, love, and more love, that's the only thing that works. Not sorta love, but genuine, real love. If you have the chance to be there for your child, and for your family, nothing else will ever be more important. <u>Remember, the male is the provider and protector. Remember men, how important that role is, just don't lose sight of why you are doing it. Remember, the woman is the nurturer and nest builder.</u>

<u>Women, don't ever, ever, give that role up.</u> For both men and women when you look back, give yourself a pat on the back for a job well done. You'll never regret it. It will be the most satisfying thing you've ever done.

LOVE IS ALL THERE IS.
I LOVE MY FAMILY.

I AM HERE NOT TO TEACH YOU, BUT TO LOVE YOU.
LOVE ITSELF, WILL TEACH YOU.

Yes, We Will Have A Woman President

There will be a woman, in the White House, as president. We've been creating that reality with our thoughts (samskaras) for many years, so it will happen. There are other reasons why we will have a woman president. Women are much more organized today than men. We've also been strengthening our girls for years with masculine energy and now they're adults. The biggest reason is, we've weakened our men to the point, that as adults, they are, in many cases, acting like little boys. All one has to do is watch and listen to our politicians. It appears that they're in a three ring circus instead of in government. It's going to be harder and harder to find a real man to run for president in the future, unless he's a woman.

If we continue on this path, we will move past equality into role reversal. Leadership of feminine energy, for a short period of time, might be good for the country. We certainly aren't bringing up many men, that nowadays, are balanced enough to run. But, on a long term basis, a strong feminine energy could be very damaging to this country. Why? Because, in my opinion, men will not follow women over a long period of time. Since the male is the natural protector of his land, and since men will be ruling most other countries, the respect of leadership from near and afar will go way down. It is possible that this country could be weakened and fall, due to an extended female leadership.

That's one of the dangers of not teaching the boys to be strong, centered, male figures. How does the boy learn to be a good person? Mostly from his mother and the women. If the mother's not in the home, the country will continue to become more chaotic. If the father and the men do not take the time to strengthen the boy's protector role, the boy will be weak. The role models will become increasingly reversed, being now set by an off balanced example. Don't forget, the woman does not set the order in the way things work. She is the subtle, powerful energy; the battery in the flashlight; the powerful, supportive role.

IF THE MAN GOES OUT OF BALANCE, THE WOMAN, OVER TIME, WILL GO OUT OF BALANCE. It is the man that sets the tone. A strong male figure keeps the circle in proper order.

The above is also true for religion. In my opinion, if the leadership goes to the feminine energy, the men, on a long term basis, will not follow. It is the male that needs to be kept in balance. (Remember the chapter Divine Mother.) If the men do not follow, eventually the women will not follow.

RELIGION, IN MY OPINION, WAS SET UP MUCH
MORE TO KEEP <u>MEN</u> IN BALANCE.

Three Personal Stories

So many divorces occur when the woman works for money. Today many women are determined to be independent. They have more degrees, more education, and have set their priorities for making money higher than they were years ago. What they have forgotten is that other part of them, which in most is so strong, the goal of getting married and having a family. When a couple does get married, the woman has got to go into the supportive role otherwise a power struggle, or role reversal will eventually occur. If that happens divorce is usually just around the corner. For the marriage to survive the woman has to let go of the masculine energy she has acquired and the man will have to let go of the feminine energy he has acquired.

The woman needs lots of hugs. She needs to be kept in her feminine energy, otherwise she will explode and want to get out of the marriage. The man needs to feel like the man.

Both have to talk about their feelings, being able to fully express their needs without being shut down by the other person.

Both man and woman have to be there to help each other through the tough times, to keep the circle intact, and to keep it as stable as possible. They should love each other unconditionally and understand each other's needs.

The following are three personal stories that will illustrate some of the above points. As you start to understand the energy circle, you will be able to add to these stories. Just remember, it takes two people to make things work well, or two people to make a relationship fail. We have to take responsibility for our 50% of the energy circle. Both people have to understand and be willing to work on the energy circle, keeping the relationship strong, and never giving up.

Personal Story One

My own experience is interesting, and is a good example of how the energy circle can get out of sync. I was married a total of 18 years. I didn't know what I know today, but I had a strong father, so I always held my ground as a man so the energy circle stayed balanced. It was always a struggle for balance because my wife came from parents where the mother was very strong. Even though my marriage had its ups and downs like most marriages, it worked. (My wife always played a supportive role and is the mother of our two children.)

In about the twelfth year things were not the same. We had no choice but to take our business strengths, and in the marriage join efforts and become business partners, as well as being husband and wife. My wife agreed to the added responsibility plus most household duties, including paying the bills etc.. She was my assistant, ran the house totally, as well as being the mother and the wife. All I did as a salesman was sell, she did the rest. In five years we had amassed a lot of money. We bought an apartment building, had a pension plan, were now a business corporation, and were climbing the ladder of financial success. We even went out to dinner and had corporate meetings. She was spending time with accountants, attorneys, and bankers. She was beginning to explode and I had lost reality. I have to admit it, I didn't see the divorce coming. But I sure did help set it up. We needed to hire an assistant, and she needed to get back into her feminine energy. She wanted to get paid for her work. The money was always for her and our children. Instead of me buying her flowers and feminine things to keep her in balance I watched her get more and more stressed out, and off balance. Remember, I didn't know what I know today. Her masculine energy was increasing; her feminine energy was getting weaker. There was a huge void left in the circle. At the same time, the kids were getting older. Her perception was, she was moving towards the forest dweller stage, even though the kids were only 13 and 15 years old. The energy circle was beginning to shatter. She didn't feel like a woman anymore.

You may have lived a similar experience, or know of people who have. Please tell them to read this book.

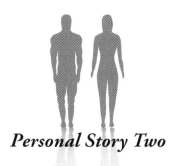

Personal Story Two

My next story is about this young couple I know. This story is very close to me, because it's about my own daughter. Meeting a man is not easy. Her relationships were not working, mostly because the men were too weak and my daughter was too strong. We talked about that. I was coming to the conclusion that there were no true men, or not many, but that if she met a nice guy, with her feminine energy directed properly, she could strengthen the male energy. My daughter and I always talked a lot together. We would talk about anything and everything. Since I was acquiring all this spiritual, holistic knowledge that had helped her in the past, she understood what I was saying. Well, she met a nice guy, and like many young men, he was getting his act together. His credit was lousy; his earnings were low, but he was headed in the right direction, and he was a good guy. That's important. My daughter and he decided to live together, so they went to look for an apartment. She automatically thought about colors and decorating. The nurturing role. He automatically looked at the way the place was built, making sure the place was safe enough for his girlfriend. The protector role. That's the natural thing to do.

They decided to take a certain apartment that they had agreed upon. One day my daughter and I were talking. She told me that the lease was driving her crazy. It just didn't read the way it was supposed to. I tried to ask her why she was handling the lease. She said, "Dad, leave me alone!" Another day, she told me that they were buying some furniture, and were going to put it on her credit card. I tried to talk to my daughter. She said, "Dad, leave me alone!" Don't forget, the woman can go into the masculine energy fairly well, it's just that life is tougher that way. So, she had credit, but she wanted a relationship. She wanted to marry this man. They had been living together a few months when I got a call. "Dad, I need to talk to you. "Okay," I said, "but will you listen to what I have to say?" "Yes," she said. My daughter came over to my house. What had happened was her boyfriend had stopped working. I asked her if she would like to know what was going on. "Yes" she said. This is what I told her. "You've pulled the masculine energy out from under him. He doesn't feel much like a man, and subconsciously wants out of the relationship." "What do I do," she said. "You have to let go of your masculine energy. He is the protector of the relationship, not you. Let him pay the rent, and you pay your share to him and get that furniture charge out of your name as fast as you possibly can. He can't be paying you for the furniture every month." How she handled it exactly, I don't know, but she did it quickly. He proposed within months. They had a traditional wedding with traditional marriage vows. They now have a beautiful family, a beautiful home, and a beautiful life. They keep the circle balanced naturally today, but don't take anything for granted. One always has to remember that the circle does exist.

Personal Story Three

My own parents had a wonderful marriage. My mother died at almost 91. My father is 92 as this book is being written. Nobody's life is without difficulties, but a lot of the problems we set up for ourselves. As I've said before, my mother was the smart one and the strength of the family, but it took us a long time to understand that. When she died, we could feel that a tremendous amount of magnetic energy had left.

My dad flipped for her right away. My mother said she married him because he was a nice person. They were married 66 years. When my father and mother married, she had a job; my father wasn't working. It was the depression. My mother was there for him on a supportive level always, and was always the wife. My father got a job. One day I asked him why he did what he did to make a living. He said, "I was married, I had responsibilities." I don't think my mother ever worked for money again. My father sometimes is, and was, a pain in the neck, but one thing I know, he loved my mother and loved my sister and me. My mother was there for all of us as a wife and a mother, always. My father was there for all of us, as a husband and a father, always. When I was younger we lost everything financially. We had to sell our home. My father still says today, that when we sold that home he felt terrible; my mom loved that home. My mother was the one that helped my father get started again. She was always the mother, always the wife. She was always there for me, my sister, and my father. My father says they never fought. I remember voices being raised, but not often. I'm not saying they were perfect, but I sure wouldn't trade my childhood for anyone elses. My parents never swore and they were always there for each other. My mother played the supportive role, always. My father was always the man. My mother was never a threat to my father's masculine energy. When we grew up, my mother worked for charitable organizations; she never earned any money.

One day my mother had a stroke. The circle was on the verge of short circuiting. My mother was only a small portion of the circle now. She was always a wonderful wife. My parents were in their seventies. My mother was very ill. My father had another job, another career was started. Without any question, he quit his job, and took care of my mother from that point on. For fifteen years he was a cook, dietician, maid, nurse, physical therapist, hairdresser, and chauffeur. He did anything it took to keep her as comfortable as possible, and to keep her alive. She lived longer than she probably should have, because he was there for her every minute. He never quit loving her, ever. He refused to put her in a nursing home, even when the energy circle was almost all him. We were all there for her, because she was always there for us, always. What she taught us and the love that she had for us, will be there forever. My mother's strong power is recognized now, more than ever before. In her feminine energy, was her tremendous, super, incredible strength. We were not rich, money wise, and my father wished he could have given my mother more. As I get older, I realize we were the wealthiest of all!

Important Information

Don't always believe people when you ask them how they are. It's almost like a reflex action to say, "fine." Their words may not be the truth.

A person that is divorced may say one thing and feel the other. Don't forget, in a divorce, the energy circle has become shattered.

Divorces can cause suicides, deaths, incurable diseases for both adults and children, nervous breakdowns, drug and alcohol problems, and many people going into therapy for the rest of their lives. <u>I have seen some of these problems cured over time from just plain LOVE, and never, ever, giving up. Not tough love, real love from the heart.</u>

Two existing energy circles that join, will not be perfectly round, but at best, be shaped like an egg, and will wobble.

Manipulation and control have no place in a relationship. Only honesty of thoughts and feelings and love will work.

What a person plants, that person will eventually harvest.

A marriage is a joining of spirit to spirit, flesh to flesh, brain to brain. Why is it that we take a marriage so lightly?

Every action creates a reaction.

The Right Person

We get married to a person and a few years later we get divorced. Perhaps we live with someone for a few months or years and the relationship breaks up. We give the excuse that they weren't the right person. Well, maybe not. The question is, how could we have chosen a better mate?

You've already read that we have to take our share of the responsibility for a relationship or marriage not working. I hope the following few pointers on how to pick a mate will help.

1. You must feel the magic inside of you. That chemistry is something we don't understand, but if there, it will always be there.
2. He or she should be a balance to your energy. Opposites attract.
3. Be with a like-minded person. Having a lot in common just makes things easier.
4. Don't try to fix anyone. If you want to be a fixer, be their friend, not their spouse.
5. If you want to know what a person will be like, check out their parents. A seed doesn't drop too far from the tree.
6. A person should be willing to communicate, say I'm sorry, I love you, hug, cry, and be willing to go for good help in times of crisis. A person should be willing to work through problems and keep commitments.
7. A man should be willing to prove right from the beginning, that he will take responsibility for his side of the circle, and the woman should automatically show that she is willing to take responsibility for her side.

8. <u>Communication and support for each other should always be there.</u>

** Remember, if the energy circle is in balance, you have a good chance to touch the furthest star.**

If you get married or are married remember:
MARRIAGE IS A LIFE-LONG COMMITMENT. DON'T GET MARRIED WITH THE IDEA THAT IF IT DOESN'T WORK YOU WILL GET OUT.

4 Steps To Dating

1. You meet someone.
2. You date someone.
3. You become somewhat intimate.
4. Consummation of the relationship.

Very rarely, if the above steps go out of order, will a relationship have a strong foundation and wind up in marriage. If you go out of sync, you will have to go back to the beginning, set up the steps in the proper order, and start again to create a solid relationship.

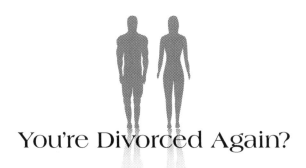

You're Divorced Again?

How many times do you meet people that have been divorced two, three times, or maybe more? It seems to be commonplace. Sometimes, a second bad choice is made. I think though, that, that is rarely the true reason. We get divorced again, because we haven't changed ourselves. Whatever our pattern is, we continue to repeat it, which means that our first marriage would probably have worked if we had looked at ourselves and not blamed the other person. I have noticed this over and over again, and yet people aren't willing to look at themselves in the mirror and say, "I need to work on myself and make myself better." Stop pointing the finger out there, and turn the finger towards you. A true annulment is a rare thing to get, which means that the true need for separation is also very rare. The divorce rate is over 50%. That's way too much, and it has to mean that people are doing things for the wrong reason, not thinking clearly. Divorce, generally is not the answer, and the destruction to the family is usually devastating.

DON'T GET A DIVORCE; MAKE YOUR MARRIAGE WORK!

Man, Oh Man

On July 15th, 1999 this front page headline appeared in one of the local newspaper.

<u>**WORKING MOM GETS KIDS.**</u>
<u>**Stay-at-home dad blames gender bias in ruling on girls.**</u>

This man was a Mr. Mom. Men, you are the provider and protector of your families, and don't you forget that. Always remember who you are, and don't get caught up in the upside down world of today. This man was a good father, but that didn't make one bit of difference.

The woman should have been at home raising the kids, and he needed to be at work. A role reversal relationship will always short circuit. Someone has to explode and everybody loses.

REMEMBER TO KEEP THE ENERGY CIRCLE IN BALANCE. IT'S REALLY IMPORTANT!

Perfectly Clear

I want everyone's life to be better. Wouldn't that be nice? I've seen so much hurt out there, much of it because we lack the truth as to what our birthright roles are. This book is trying to get you to think. If I've pushed your buttons, I've done my job. If you're discussing this information with your spouse or a friend, I've done my job. If you don't agree with me, and discuss that disagreement with someone, then I've also done my job.

We aren't being taught properly, I've said that. We need to allow our partners to express their feelings, and not shut them down. We need to understand that they're not crazy or wrong, that they are talking about their feelings. We need to be totally honest with each other. The truth always needs to be said in order for others to understand the picture that we paint when we talk. Otherwise, there are pieces missing, or that don't fit the picture. Without a complete, truthful picture, how is the other person ever to fully understand and properly respond?

When I talk about women staying at home for their families, it's because the loss is tremendous if they don't. If a woman doesn't need to work, she shouldn't. We all have too much "stuff". The sad truth is we all don't get enough love. Stuff will never make anyone happy, except on a short term basis. For all the women that are educated please teach the children what you've learned. I know some of you have gone to school for many years. It's only the ego that needs the gratification of using your education in the work place. You can always go back to work when the kids grow up, if you want to. The children really need you at home.

Set a good example for your kids, otherwise, when they get married, they may treat their children just the way you treated them. One thing they might do is leave their kids with someone else, and that person will never love them as much as you do. As a grandparent, I don't think you'll like that, and you'll wish you had set a better example. On top of that, your child may not have time for you, if you weren't there for them.

For the men, making a living is only part of your responsibility. It is important to show love to your family and to spend time with them. Your daughter needs you. Your son needs you. Your wife needs you. Sure, you want them to have everything, but if they don't feel they have your love, then they have nothing. Not only do they need your time and love, they need to hear your words, such as I LOVE YOU. Men never say that enough, or, many times, not at all.

The energy circle really is there, and when properly understood, will make your life wonderful.

Remember the FOREST DWELLER STAGE OF LIFE? In it we start to make a natural shift as our responsibilities change. Our children don't need us as much, because they are on the way out or have already left the energy circle. Now it's time to turn our focus toward society as a whole; the desire to serve, love, and give to humanity now automatically increases. At this stage it's not important to earn a lot of money, unless you have to; it is important to make a difference. It's still very important for the adults, in the forest dweller stage, to continue to be proper role models, but the focus widens. Now it's time to help those that are in need. If we didn't do that before, now is the time to do it. We need to teach what we've learned to the younger generation, so that they will be able to live a good life, and then they will teach the next generation when they, themselves, reach the forest dweller stage.

Ladies please don't forget to be there for the man in your life. He needs your love and support.

TRUTH OVERCOMES ALL ERROR.

Grounded

When the energy circle is functioning properly, when both masculine and feminine energies are working the way they were meant to, both people should feel very much in balance. A feeling of bliss, or calmness, should pretty much prevail.

WHERE THERE IS LOVE, THERE IS PEACE AND HARMONY.

To The Kids

This is the final chapter that I need to write to tell my story. I almost didn't write it. Some of you kids are making a lot of noise, too violent for me. I just cry inside my heart. You are our future men and women. Hopefully, you'll be smarter than your parents were. Oh, I don't mean in an academic way, I mean being emotionally smarter. I mean being in touch with the truth, and setting examples of love, and solving problems without violence.

Understand, that each <u>so called</u> disappointment or mistake, will move you forward towards your goal. Each person and experience that comes into your life will teach you something. Never look at anything as a failure, and never, ever, give up, as long as what you are doing comes from your heart. You, may just turn out to be one of the greatest people ever to have set foot on this planet!

Young people have always fought for change, and you're no different. We need change, and we need you to help us do that. You are right, our schools are empty of love, our homes are empty of love. The movies, television, newspapers, and magazines, are all spewing out mostly negative information. Much of what we see and hear in the media contains sex and violence.

What you're trying to teach us, is that there's an emptiness inside of you, and you're exploding from it. There are three parts to us; we are all body, mind, and spirit. Without our spirit, we are nothing but a big, hollow machine. What has happened is that you feel empty. You're not allowed to connect with your True Self in school; the adults have seen to that. Homes have less love in them than they used to, and people have less religion in their homes, so there is little to no connection with the spirit there! Very few people have time to read a spiritual book anymore. So, the most important part of you, your spirit, is being neglected, and you're crying out. Your way today is the way the adults are teaching you. You're crying out in violence, hatred, lust and greed.

It's time to speak out and tell the adults that you don't want any more of their garbage (poor examples). Tell them to stop the killing, the abuse, the swearing, the anger, the sex without love, the dishonesty and cheating for gain; they are certainly not making anyone's life better.

EVERY STEP IN YOUR LIFE WILL LEAD TO THE NEXT STEP!

Kids, let me tell you a story

There was a man born two thousand years ago. He was born in a barn early in the morning. Nobody even knew about his birth, or cared, except three spiritually connected people who came to see him and to honor his arrival to earth. His parents were poor people, not well educated, but people of substance, good values. His parents gave him a lot of love; that was his wealth. There was so much love in his heart that when he grew up he had to talk about it.

As a child he was probably like all of you kids. He probably played like you play. I'm sure he fell, and got cuts and bruises, just the same as you. His parents couldn't afford to send him to college, and I don't even know if he graduated high school, but inside him was a heart of gold. He did have a spiritual and religious education. He didn't have any degrees or diplomas. He didn't write any books to show us how smart he was. He was smart from inside with clear thought. When he spoke, he spoke from his heart and people listened. Even in his last few days of living on this planet he was still teaching, still loving. Remember, he never got an A, no plaques up on the wall. He didn't have a lot of money or fancy designer clothes. I'm not so sure he ever cared if anyone remembered his name, but everybody does. **Everybody!!!!!!!!!!**

Now kids, it's important to graduate high school, and maybe college. It's important to learn all you can. It's important to make a positive difference in this world. It's important to know that you did the very best that you could do. It's important that you give and live from your heart, and that you treat everyone as you would like them to treat you. No matter what your circumstances are, whether you are rich or poor, you can be the best that there is. The greatest people never, ever asked for fame and glory. They gave from their hearts, and did the very best they could. They were honest, good people that did incredible things for this experience called life. Each one of you can be the best. If you come from your heart, and never give up, that's what will happen.

Questionnaire

1- You're at a crowded party. A man and a woman are trying to get to the dance floor. Which one should go first and why?

    A- The woman should always go first.

    B- The man should go first.

    C- They should walk side by side, waving to the crowd and smiling.

2- A family of four is walking down the street; the husband, wife and their two children. A man comes out of the dark about 25 feet away, and points a gun. The family has one second to react before the gun is fired. What will instinctively happen and why?

    A- The man is the protector and will, from instinct, jump in front of the entire family.

    B- Everyone will run away as fast as they can.

    C- The woman will protect the husband at all costs, not even thinking about the kids.

3- A man and a woman enter a movie theatre and sit down. Which one enters the row of seats first and why?

    A- Usually the man, he wants to make sure all is safe down the aisle.

    B- The woman goes in first most of the time.

    C- Both fight over the same seat.

4- What is the difference between a man who cooks at work, and a man who cooks at home?

    A- A man who cooks at work is being the provider. If a man cooks at home the man may be intruding on the womans' nurturing role.

    B- The man will cook better food at home.

    C- None of these.

5- A man and woman are walking down the street. Who would normally walk on the outside and why?

    A- The male is the protector. Normally, he would walk on the curbside to protect the woman.

    B- The woman should walk on the outside; it just makes more sense.

    C- No one should care one way or the other.

6- A major storm has hit, and all the electrical power goes out. There are trees everywhere that need to be cut and towed away. Who will do the heavy, hard labor?

    A- The woman will usually do the heavy labor. After all, why not?

    B- Just leave the mess there. Someone will eventually clean it up.

    C- The man, as the protector, will do the heavy lifting, and cut and tow the trees away. I hope so, anyhow.

7- When a man and woman dance, who does the leading and why?

    A- Who cares, it's not important.

    B- The male is the enfolder/protector. It just feels right when the male leads.

    C- The woman should definitely lead.

8- When a man and woman lay in bed which one generally cuddles into the other and why?

    A- The man

    B- The woman

    C- Neither

9- If a man and woman are stranded on some dark road, who will take the leadership position and why?

A- Hopefully, the woman will take charge, as she is the leader of the family.

B- Hopefully he will. By now you know A is incorrect, so it must be B.

C- All of the above

10- When a woman goes to buy a car, other than money, generally what is she most concerned about?

A- Design and color.

B- How many seconds it take to get from 0-60 mph, and the size of the tires.

C- All of the above

11- When a woman gets a flat tire, how many women do you know that want to change that tire and why?

A- None

B- None

C- All of the above

12- When the man and woman are side by side and they put their arms around each other, where should each one place their arm?

A- The male's arm on the woman's shoulder. The woman's arm around the man's waist.

B- The woman's arm around the male's shoulder. The man's arm around the woman's waist

C- Does it really matter?

13- There is only one seat left on the bus. Who should take the seat?

A- The seat should be left empty just in case a lone person gets on the bus.

B- The young man, he's had a hard day.

C- The woman, after all the man is the protector.

There are so many other questions to ask. These are only a few. How many can you think of?

ANSWERS ARE ON NEXT PAGE

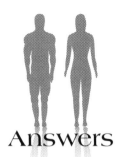

Answers

1B- The man should go first. The man should part the crowd so that the woman can walk through easily. The male is the protector.

2A- Instinctively, the woman will jump in front of the children. The man will jump in front of the entire family and take the bullet. The male is a natural protector to the entire family. If the man was not there, the woman would take the bullet.

3B- The woman goes in first to be protected from anyone walking down the aisle. If the inside seat is next to someone else, and the woman is uncomfortable, or if someone in front is too tall to see over, then the woman might want to switch. In any case the male is the protector.

4A- A male is the provider, and a chef earns money to take care of his family. At home, under normal circumstances, cooking is a nurturing role. If the woman is unable to cook, or needs help at home, then the man will cook as more of a protector role.

5A- It's only common sense that the man would usually walk on the curbside. He is the protector and needs to do whatever is necessary to make sure that she is protected as much as possible.

6C- The power is out, so it's all hard physical labor. Generally the man is stronger on a physical level and will do the lifting. The woman will probably assist on a more supportive level. (Technology has made things easier, but that doesn't mean that anything has really changed.)

7B- Of course, it's the male. What woman wants to take the lead, or will think much of the male if she is able to do so?

88- The woman usually cuddles into the man. He is enfolding her. Sometimes if he has a tough day he may need to cuddle into her, but I'm sure if he were to do so on a regular basis, she would not be very happy.

98- Hopefully, he will. Being the protector, the male should have the courage and strength to do so. A woman wants to feel secure. She does not really want to be with a wimp, ever, but certainly not now.

10A- When buying a car the woman is usually more interested in color and design. The male certainly is more interested in engine size and performance.

11C- None. I never met a woman yet, that on the side of a road, or in a parking lot, or anywhere for that matter, wants to jack up the car, lift a heavy tire, get filthy and sweaty, and then say, "Am I happy I did that!" On the other hand, the male wants to help. It's his protector role, and makes him feel good that he could do it.

12A- The man's arm will generally be around the woman's shoulder, her arm around his waist. This way the man has the leverage to enfold/protect.

13C- The woman. It has to be, but, probably the young man will take the seat, if he can get it. Many young women don't want to be treated like women anymore, so why should he care? And probably, no one's taught him. I sure hope someone has.

HOW DID YOU DO? There are many more questions we can all think of, but the answers are all the same. The male is the provider and protector of his mate and family. The woman is the nurturer and nest builder for her mate and family. I hope you enjoyed taking this quiz.

MY BEST FRIEND
IS THE ONE
WHO BRINGS OUT
THE BEST IN ME

Henry Ford

(The person one marries does become one's best friend.

Let them bring out the best in you.)

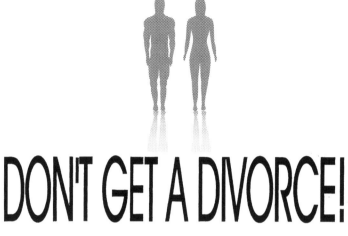

DON'T GET A DIVORCE!

LOVE EACH OTHER INSTEAD

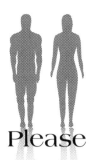

Please

To you women and warriors, this message is for you. I watch some of you, on television and in the movies. Some of you appear in newspapers and magazines. Some of you are famous; you're actresses, actors, or executives of major companies. You record records, your're anchor people of news shows, you're famous athletes, and some of you are recognized politicians. You are definitely famous role models. People look up to you. You're setting an example. People think if I could be just like them, live my life just like them, I'd be the happiest person ever. The children are greatly influenced by what they see and hear from you, and many of them want to be just like you.

My question to you is, are you really happy? My other question is, how much of your life did you sacrifice to do what you're doing. Since you are so influential, you have to tell the truth. In fact, everyone has to tell the truth, because society is sliding backwards, thinking that it is moving forwards. What an illusion.

Men and women, we are on a steep decline; don't you feel it? Just pick up the newspapers and watch the news. For the strong women role models, were you there for your kids? Are your kids okay today? If you put your job ahead of everything, do you wish you hadn't? For those men that are so influential, tell the truth about your life. How did your kids do? Are you people married? Did you get divorced because you were never home, never had time for your family?

WHETHER YOU LIKE IT OR NOT, PEOPLE LOOK UP TO YOU, THEY RESPECT YOU, AND THEY FOLLOW YOU. You have to tell the truth. If you don't, not only will you have failed, maybe those who follow you will too. If you had successes, tell what you did to have them. If you sacrificed for them, tell us. **The next generation of adults is counting on you!**

The Book And Me

I had to write it. We are being so misled. Adults are being clobbered, and children are being clobbered. I have two children, grown up now, and I'm still dealing with the past. Divorce ruined a terrific family. I have seen so much sadness since my divorce, in my life, and in so many other people's lives, that how could I not try to tell what I've learned?

It's like God dropped a bombshell in my life and then said: *"Explain to people what I am teaching you. I'm not happy you are divorced, but at least get the knowledge out. I will move you forward. A lot of what I give you will not be pleasant, but it will teach you. Make sure you teach it. Get it out there. Don't give up; get the message out. I do not like what is happening to My teachings. I do not like what is happening to the way I designed men and women to live. I gave your forefathers very specific instructions on how you were to function, but again, I notice how few are listening. I am happy there are those that are doing their best to keep their marriage intact. I know they, and their children, will be better for it.*

I am not happy that you are divorced, and never will be. You know, until then, I always made your life good. That's over. Your life is to be dedicated to helping others. This is My commandment to you. Understand, that I am with you on this, and only this. Helping others follow My laws is the only thing that will now work for you.

The book you have written is good. It's not perfect, but it will get people to think. I want people to think. I want people to think how they have forgotten and have disconnected from Me. I want people to know that

I made a marriage a sacrament, a way to achieve happiness, a way for the next generation to grow up happy. I designed you humans in a certain way. To fool around with My design is to make a chaotic mess out of things. Just look at the children. How can they be okay, if you're not? It takes two to raise a family, not one. It takes a whole community to raise a community, not just a few. I look at those that are not taking their marriage seriously, and I shudder and shake My head in disgust. Sometimes, those shudders appear in violent storms and earthquakes. When you people get your act together, I will take care of things. If you keep messing things up, and abusing one another, if you have lost respect for Me, and Mother Earth, then I will not be there as a parent, nor will I take your disrespect lightly. You can do what you want, but that does not mean that I give My approval. I am signing off now; thank you again for listening to Me. Please understand that I am always watching and listening. I want your life to be wonderful. I've made it easy, just do it. Follow My laws and I will be there for you. With all my love ------------------------"

THE END
OR
MAYBE IT'S JUST THE BEGINNING

The Woman And The Warrior

WOMAN

YOU ARE THE MAKER OF THE FAMILY.
YOU ARE THE MAKER OF THE NATION.
YOU ARE THE MAKER OF THE WORLD.
THE FUTURE OF THE WORLD IS
ENTIRELY IN YOUR HANDS.

WARRIOR

YOU ARE AGGRESSIVE BY NATURE.
YOU ARE OUT OF BALANCE FROM BIRTH.
YOU ARE WITHOUT POWER, YET EXTREMELY POWERFUL.
YOU ARE THE DEFENDER OF THE FAMILY,
THE NATION, AND THE WORLD.

SINGLE? MARRIED? READ THIS BOOK!

Printed in the United States
By Bookmasters